DON'T TRY THIS AT HOME

DON'T TRY
THIS AT HOME

*Culinary Catastrophes from
the World's Greatest Chefs*

Edited by Kimberly Witherspoon
and Andrew Friedman

BLOOMSBURY

First published in Great Britain 2006
This paperback edition published 2007

Copyright © 2006 by Inkwell Management

The moral right of the authors has been acknowledged

Bloomsbury Publishing Plc, 36 Soho Square, London WID 3QY

A CIP catalogue record for this book
is available from the British Library

ISBN 9780747585435

Typeset by Hewer Text UK Ltd, Edinburgh
Printed in Great Britain by Clays Limited, St Ives plc

www.bloomsbury.com

To Summer and Paul

—K.W.

As always, to Caitlin, and for the first time,
to Declan and Taylor, two great kids

—A.F.

CONTENTS

Introduction		1
JAMIE OLIVER	The End of Innocence	3
MICHEL ROUX	Christmas in Paris	11
TOM AIKENS	On Second Thoughts	19
RAYMOND BLANC	Lost and Found	25
SALLY CLARKE	The 'No Choice' Life	35
ROWLEY LEIGH	The Boiling Point	41
ANTONIO CARLUCCIO	Man's Best Friend	49
SHAUN HILL	A Walk on the Moon	55
VINEET BHATIA	The Next Best Thing	63
GIORGIO LOCATELLI	An Italian in Paris	69
FERGUS HENDERSON	Genus Loci	79
TAMASIN DAY-LEWIS	Euphoria	84
SAMUEL CLARK	A Simple Request	96
ANTONY WORRALL THOMPSON	Grace under Pressure	102
HESTON BLUMENTHAL	Lean Times at the Fat Duck	106
FERRÁN ADRIÀ	Horror in Gerona	114
NEIL PERRY	Our First Friday	121
TESSA KIROS	A Secret Worth Keeping	127
BILL GRANGER	A Christmas Story	132

DAVID THOMPSON   Kitchen Basics   138

ANTHONY BOURDAIN   New Year's Meltdown   144

MICHELLE BERNSTEIN   Two Great Tastes that
                          Taste Great Together   163

MARIO BATALI   The Last Straw   170

GABRIELLE HAMILTON   The Blind Line Cook   177

PINO LUONGO   A User's Guide to Opening
                          a Hamptons Restaurant   186

ERIC RIPERT   You Really Ought to Think
                          about Becoming a Waiter   203

DANIEL BOULUD   On the Road Again   210

JIMMY BRADLEY   Ship of Fools   218

WYLIE DUFRESNE   Beastmaster   228

MARCUS SAMUELSSON   The Big Chill   238

DAVID BURKE   White Lie   247

BILL TELEPAN   Neverland   253

JONATHAN EISMANN   The Curious Case of
                          Tommy Flynn   264

Acknowledgements   273

Introduction

NEARLY 200 YEARS AGO, the legendary French gastronome Jean Anthelme Brillat-Savarin observed that 'the truly dedicated chef or the true lover of food is a person who has learnt to go beyond mere catastrophe and to salvage at least one golden moment from every meal'.

In these pages, a selection of the world's finest chefs share, in refreshingly frank detail, the stories of their biggest mishaps, missteps, misfortunes, and misadventures. To our delight, much of what they salvage goes beyond the strictly culinary.

For their honesty, we thank the chefs themselves, who may surprise you as they discuss moments they'd rather forget, bringing their stories to life with revelations of humility, self-doubt, and even shame. Disasters, especially those involving food, are funny to look back on, but can be ego-deflating when they occur – it's a credit to these chefs that they are able to be simultaneously profound and laugh-provoking.

As we consider the stories, a number of themes emerge: the fish-out-of-water syndrome that greets young cooks working and travelling abroad proves a fertile breeding ground for near-farcical scenarios. The constant struggle to find and keep good employees is another popular motif, leading to tales of everything from a blind line cook to a culinary faith-healing. Restaurants make for strange bedfellows, a truth examined in these pages via the tension between cooks and chefs and chefs and owners. Finally, the chaos that ensues when a chef leaves his or her kitchen and takes the show on the road can lead to countless unforeseen catastrophes.

For all of us, both cooks and non-cooks, this book offers its own form of hope – evidence that even those who are the very best in their chosen field, famous for exhibiting perfection on a nightly basis, can make a mistake, maybe even a disastrous one, and then laugh at it, and at themselves.

Even more reassuring is how often, and how well, they improvise a way out, finding inspiration when they need it most, and emerging victorious, even if it means sometimes telling a white lie.

'In my business, failure is not an option,' says one chef. It's one thing to say that and quite another to live it. These professionals live it on a daily basis, and we're grateful that they took time out to rummage through their memories and pick out the worst – by which we mean the 'best' – to share.

KIMBERLY WITHERSPOON
ANDREW FRIEDMAN

The End of Innocence
JAMIE OLIVER

Jamie Oliver is one of this country's most well-known and best-loved chefs. His many television series include The Naked Chef *and* Jamie's Great Italian Escape. *He has written six best-selling cookbooks, which have been published worldwide and translated into twenty-three languages. Before striking out on his own, Jamie worked at the Neal Street Restaurant and the River Café. In November 2002, he opened the restaurant Fifteen, in London's Hoxton, the subject of the television documentary,* Jamie's Kitchen. *Two more Fifteen restaurants have since opened in Amsterdam and Cornwall, and plans for further restaurants are in the making. As a direct result of the television programme,* Jamie's School Dinners, *which highlighted the abysmal quality of school food in Britain, the Government promised to increase the school budget for food by £280 million. In 2000, Jamie married his childhood sweetheart, Jools. They have two daughters.*

'FRY, YOU BASTARD.'

These three words were the first I remember hearing from a restaurant kitchen, and they made such an impression on me. They shaped my view of the mostly abnormal people attracted to the strange, punishing, and freewheeling world of professional cooking!

At the time my family lived in a flat over my parents' pub in a 450-year-old building. I was six years old when the words travelled up from the kitchen through the paper-thin floors into our living room.

'Fry, you bastard.'

I could tell from the strange intonation – a sort of half-conscious mumbling – that they were coming from a tall boy – let's call him Gerry – who worked in the place and who I saw coming and going nearly every day of my young life.

But, though I knew whose voice I was hearing, I had no idea what he was referring to.

I was also puzzled by the strange little buzzing sound, short but unmistakably electric, that followed the words.

What is that? I wondered each time he spoke, my curiosity growing almost unbearable.

Again, it came: 'Fry, you bastard.' Followed by that zippy little buzz.

I couldn't take it any more. I had to know what Gerry was up to.

I ran down the stairs into the pub. As it was very early in the morning, there was nobody around. On tiptoes, I made my way to the kitchen, pushed open the doors, and looked inside.

There was Gerry, standing at a work station, busy peeling and marinading a load of prawns. But he was obviously getting a bit bored and every so often, instead of adding a newly peeled prawn to the bowl of marinade, he'd hold it up and say to it, 'Fry, you bastard,' then flick it across the room into the fly killer – one of those caged, electrified neon bars that zaps insects dead on contact.

As the shellfish hit the glowing tube, it made the buzzing sound I'd been hearing all morning. On the floor was a pile of blackened prawns. I learnt something that day that I would come to fully appreciate as I began *my* life in this profession: that you get some real characters in a professional kitchen!

My education in the kitchen began early. By the age of seven I was working in the pub, and the other guys taught me all about the practical jokes that were to become part and parcel of my life in the kitchen. Like the night we took poor Gerry's leather jacket, soaked it in water, hung it in the freezer, then returned it to the coat rack, so that when he went to put it on at the end of the evening, after working hard for more than twelve hours and ready to go home, it was rock hard and as cold as ice.

I learnt to dish out practical jokes, and I learnt to take them as well. Because I was quite small, I often found myself locked in the freezer or tossed into the fish sink with all the stinking bits. Nice!

Before long, I took this as a fact of life. And I'll tell you a secret: I *loved* it. Almost as much as the food itself, I loved the guys who played these jokes on me and made me feel part of their team.

I've never been disappointed. No matter where I've worked, there's always been lots of fun, harmless teasing and practical jokes.

When I started college in London, I did some work experience in a hotel. *Everyone* in that kitchen was stark raving mad, from the ex-military head chef to the line cook who came to work decked out as a teddy boy in platform shoes, a long blue felt jacket, and a huge belt buckle. He blasted music from the portable radio at his station and performed *every* task, even peeling little vegetables, with an enormous chef's knife. Now, *that*'s rock and roll!

This is where I learnt that pranks didn't have to be confined to the kitchen. Havoc could be caused by preying on the waiting staff who, let's face it, were more civilised, and therefore easier pickings for the likes of us kitchen blokes than we were for each other.

There was a female manager in that hotel restaurant who was the constant target of the teddy boy. Every afternoon at about the same time, she'd come into the kitchen to borrow the wine-cellar key from him. One day, in preparation for this ritual, he warmed two kidneys on a steel hotel plate. When he heard her coming down the stairs at the usual time, he got me to drop the kidneys into his trouser pocket.

He then hoisted up two prep trays loaded with food and turned round just as the manager made it to the foot of the stairs.

'May I have the key, please,' she said.

'Of course,' he replied, indicating that she should get the key from his pocket.

She stuck her hand in and made a horrified face, clearly thinking that he had a hole in his pocket and that instead of the key she had got herself a handful of warm bollocks! Thankfully she saw the funny side of it after she'd got over the shock.

Now, you might think this is unacceptable behaviour, and you're right, of course. But it was harmless, and we'd all be great friends afterwards.

Lest you think it's all fun and games, there are times when these schoolboy pranks are employed for a very good reason.

I have a pet peeve. I can't stand it when people nick food from my station. So when other chefs take this liberty, I always get my revenge!

Like the Aussie who worked with me in an Italian restaurant. I was the pastry chef and he was always grabbing my biscuits as he passed by, or taking a spoon out of his pocket and dipping it, repeatedly, into my sauces and ice creams.

This really annoyed me.

Well, the kitchen had a box of seriously hot Sicilian bell peppers that were fruity and delicious, but also quite lethal in large quantities. I helped myself to some and puréed them so they looked like a berry sauce. I layered this into a glass with some ice cream and asked the Aussie if he'd like to try our new 'Tuscan parfait'.

'I'd love to!' he exclaimed and grabbed a large spoon.

He scooped up a huge mouthful of the topping and crammed it into his mouth. Beads of sweat instantly appeared on his forehead as he swallowed some. He managed to spit out about half the stuff, then looked at me with red eyes. 'You bastard,' he shouted at me. 'I lived in Asia for years and I can take that spicy . . .' As the chilli took hold, he trailed off and began gasping for air, leaning on the counter of my station.

All the other chefs stopped working and came over to watch.

A minute or two went by and then he collapsed on the floor

and began shaking. His face was numb and he literally could not stand back up.

I spent the evening performing his kitchen duties *and* mine, all the while nursing him back to health by making him gargle milk and helping him to pull strips of skin out of his mouth. He was fine by the end of the night and I apologised, because I truly never meant to hurt him. But I wasn't really all that sorry. I guess we both learnt a lesson – and he never nicked any of my food again.

Over the years I have come to realise that not everyone appreciates the fun and games of the kitchen, though . . . And the thing I enjoy doing the most – moonies – are often the *least* appreciated by those who don't share the chefs' sense of humour.

Like the waitress at the River Café who was studying photography. In our very trusting environment at the restaurant, nobody locked his or her locker.

Big mistake.

One day, while this waitress was on the service floor, we took her camera and snapped sixteen photos of the lot of us doing moonies – real rugby-player-after-game stuff. Needless to say, when she took the film to her very proper, very professional lab, the technicians were amused, but she was not.

But the person I offended the most was a Portuguese clean-up man who I'll call Arturo. He was a nervous sort, not unlike Manuel, the character from the TV show *Fawlty Towers*. My mentor, Gennaro, and I were working together at this restaurant – he was the pasta man and I was the pastry chef. And while we loved to cook, nothing made us happier than making Arturo jump.

Gennaro used to do this by dropping a stack of steel trays when Arturo's back was turned. They would clatter really loudly and Arturo would leap in the air, his nerves completely on edge.

My approach was a bit more crude. At the end of the night, Arturo had to pull all the industrial refrigerators out from the wall in order to mop behind them. The units formed little corridors where I loved to taunt him. I'd stand at the end of a refrigerator-corridor, drop my trousers, bend over, slap my backside, and yell, 'Hey, Arturo, kiss my arse.'

Arturo would try to kick me as I took off, running and laughing.

One day, he was mopping up and Gennaro said, 'Go on, give him a moonie.'

As ever, I couldn't resist. I turned round and dropped my trousers. 'Hey, Arturo, kiss my arse,' I said, slapping my bare bottom.

This time, he was ready. Rather than trying to kick me, he managed to smack me with the wet mop . . . right where it hurts . . . And, believe me, it hurt like hell! I learnt my lesson and never pulled a moonie ever again. Lots of other stuff, yes, but never another moonie!

What do you eat for breakfast?
Nice fruit and a croissant from the Flour Station.

What dish would you cook in order to seduce someone?
Any whole fish roasted with lovely herbs.

What do you never cook?
Poached eggs.

What's the one dish you find hard to get right?
Poached eggs.

Christmas in Paris
MICHEL ROUX

Brought up in England, and son of legendary chef Albert Roux, Michel Roux worked in a number of kitchens in France, London, and Hong Kong before becoming Chef of Roux Restaurants, London, in 1985, a position in which he oversaw the kitchens of Roux Patisserie, Roux Lamartine, Le Poulbot Brasserie, and Le Gamin. In 1991, he became chef de cuisine of Le Gavroche, which was founded in 1967 by his father and uncle. Under his auspices, Le Gavroche has received numerous honours, including the Award of Excellence of the Carlton London Restaurant Awards, the Restaurateurs' Restaurant of the Year Award, and the Moët et Chandon London Restaurant Award for Outstanding Front of House. (Le Gavroche was also the first British restaurant to be awarded one, two, and three Michelin stars.) Roux has been a business columnist, and is the author of Le Gavroche Cookbook, The Marathon Chef, and Matching Food & Wine.

TO BE BORN into a family of chefs is never to be left
wanting for advice. My father and my uncle both believed that the best way to begin a career in the kitchen is to
immerse yourself in the world of pastry, because its necessarily
intense and exacting focus on technique fosters a discipline
that will benefit any and all cooking you do for the rest of
your life.

So it was that in 1976, at the age of sixteen, I left school in
London to travel to Paris and work in a patisserie. Not just any
patisserie: it was the best in all of France, and as such perhaps
the best in the world at the time. (Appropriately enough, the
space that once housed the shop is now home to the shop of
another pastry luminary: Pierre Hermé.)

The shop was in the Fifteenth Arrondissement on Rue Vau-
girard. It was the very model of a Parisian patisserie, a scru-
pulously clean, romantically lit marbled shrine to the art of
baking, and its sugary delights.

The chef, Maître Patissier Hellegouarche, was a big, strong,
massive bear of a man, about six feet tall, balding, with a loud
bellowing voice, which he rarely raised. He didn't have to: he
had all our respect because he led by unwavering example. He
was a true master who could perform any task in the kitchen at
the drop of a hat; a truth proved over and over again because of
his penchant for filling in personally for absent employees,
doing their jobs with joy and passion.

In short, Monsieur Hellegouarche was larger than life, a
person we thought of as you might a character in a play, or
a film, an impression heightened by his broad smile that
revealed numerous silver-covered teeth, probably from working
in such a sugar-laden environment.

The chef's wife was petite and always immaculate, exuding

the glamour, style, refinement and femininity typical of a Parisienne. She ran the front of house, and she was just as strict as her husband: in the morning, before we opened for business, her brigade of counter girls, dressed in their frilly little uniforms, lined up for inspection, whereupon Madame Hellegouarche would pass by them like a general to ensure they were just as neat and lovely as the orderly lines of pastries that filled our windows and shelves.

I learnt a lot from Monsieur Hellegouarche. Obviously, I gleaned all the promised knowledge that a pastry education was to confer upon me. Not just the technique, but also the organisation of the kitchen: located at the back of the shop, it had stainless-steel work surfaces everywhere, big baking ovens with long, pull-down doors, and a separate ice-cream-making area. There was also a cellar for items such as flour, sugar, and 50-kilo sacks of almonds that, as you'll soon learn, can be used to teach more than cooking.

But there are other, less predictable lessons one learns in two years in a kitchen like that.

For instance, all culinary students have it drilled into their heads not to be wasteful. It's one thing to be told this in a classroom and quite another to see it applied in the real world – and quite dramatically.

One Christmas the kitchen had produced an enormous amount of pear cream – about 100 litres, I'd say – in preparation for making charlottes. Two cooks were carrying the unwieldy stainless-steel vat of cream into the main walk-in refrigerator. They disappeared inside, then we heard a loud clanging, banging sound, the kind of noise that would cause any caring soul to ask, 'Is everything all right?'

We all looked over with concern just in time to see Monsieur

Hellegouarche emerge from the walk-in, covered from head to toe in pear cream.

I'm not quite sure where he'd been standing – perhaps the cooks were trying to set the vat on an inadvisably high shelf – but it was so incongruous in the otherwise perfect kitchen that we all burst out laughing.

But not Monsieur Hellegouarche. Ever the professional, he kept calm, and in his firm commander's voice, spoke from beneath the glop that encased him: 'Quickly, quickly, let's save the cream.'

Following his instructions, we each took a plastic scraper in one hand and a small bowl in the other, scraping the cream into the bowls, then passing it through a sieve into one large bowl and transferring it to a clean stainless-steel vat.

Under Monsieur Hellegouarche I also learnt that being a truly strong leader means working at least as hard as your troops.

That same Christmas, we worked a gruelling schedule. The week leading up to Christmas Day was pandemonium: we only slept four or five hours on any given night, so became more and more sleep-deprived as the 25th drew closer.

On Christmas Eve, we all worked straight through until eleven o'clock in the evening, preparing for one of the busiest days of the year.

At eleven Monsieur Hellegouarche announced, 'All right, lads: I've prepared you a meal.'

We were in disbelief. He was always there, working alongside us. How had he managed to prepare a dinner as well?

We stepped out into the public area of the shop and, amazingly, he and his wife had laid a beautiful table. I remember it as though it were yesterday: there was roast beef, potatoes, vegetables glistening with butter, and several bottles of wine, already uncorked and ready to be poured.

We sat down and ate like I imagine soldiers eat – with an intensity born of fatigue and stress – pouring and drinking an ungodly amount of wine, unabashedly helping ourselves to seconds of *everything*, and laughing hard at even the most meagre joke.

The meal only took about forty-five minutes, but it was such a pleasure to be nurtured like this. We were exhausted, but now we were ready for the onslaught of Christmas Day.

We were also ready to go home to our flats for our daily ration of sleep, but Monsieur Hellegouarche hit us with a surprise.

'OK, lads. Fifteen minutes' break, and I'll see you all back in the kitchen.'

I was shocked, but only for a moment. Because if Monsieur Hellegouarche needed me, then I was there for him – we all were – especially since we knew that he would work with us through the night.

I had a cigarette, changed into some clean whites, and baked my way into Christmas morning. The shop opened at seven, and closed at midday. I went to visit some family in Paris, and I was a zombie.

I don't remember the family visit at all, except for one detail: I didn't stay long.

Because I had to be back at work at six in the morning on the 26th.

Although Monsieur Hellegouarche preferred to lead by example, when the example didn't produce the desired behaviour, he could be quite the stern taskmaster. Nothing coaxed out the disciplinarian in him more than tardiness. He simply couldn't countenance lateness, by anyone, for any reason, and this is why I've never forgotten those gargantuan sacks of almonds.

Now, I've always considered myself responsible, even at the young age at which I arrived in Paris. But I was also a typical seventeen-year-old boy.

Each year the shop took on two apprentices, so my primary social circle consisted of myself and my contemporary, plus the two eighteen-year-olds who had been there since the previous year. The four of us lived in a flat just five minutes' walk from the shop. When we weren't immersed in pastry, we were enjoying the sheer bliss of being in a wonderful, vibrant city like Paris. We were out every night and often didn't come home at all. In fact, there was a local bar, frequented by 'ladies of the night', where we often ended our evenings, having one last drink before running off for a quick coffee *en route* to the shop.

You can live like that when you're seventeen and get away with it.

Most of the time.

The first time you were late in Monsieur Hellegouarche's shop, you got a warning. The second time, you got another warning.

If you were late a third time, then you would hear him bellow the dreaded words: 'That's it: the bag of almonds tonight is yours.'

He was referring to what was a legendary corrective measure, remembered painfully, I'm sure, by anyone who ever worked for him: your punishment was to peel an entire 50-kilo bag, and to do so *after* working a full day in the kitchen.

Twice, after late nights on the town, when I lingered too long over my morning coffee, I came running into the shop to find that the minute hand on the wall clock had cleared the hour mark. There was no point in even *hoping* that Monsieur Hellegouarche wasn't there, because *he* was always on time.

My employer would look up from his work and matter-of-factly inform me to consider myself warned.

The third time I was late – for the same reason, of course – I earned my first night with the almonds. There was no getting round it. Monsieur Hellegouarche would stay there with you to the bitter end, a logical and, I must say, admirable extension of his work ethic.

Peeling almonds is a real bastard of a job: the only way to do it is to blanch them for a few seconds in boiling water, drain them, and while they're still warm, squeeze them between your thumb and forefinger until the fleshy almond pops out of the rough brown skin.

Peeling 50 kilos of almonds takes quite a toll: after the first 25 kilos, your thumb and forefinger get raw, so numb that you need to watch your every movement, trusting your eyes in place of your diminished sense of touch.

At 35 kilos, you begin to curse yourself, because whatever it was that made you late could not possibly have been worth this torture. Had I really needed one more drink? Could I not have survived the day without my beloved coffee? How foolish!

At about 40 kilos, your fingers – and I'm not exaggerating here – begin to bleed.

By the 50th kilo, you are left with real mental and physical scars.

Most people are never late after a night with the almonds, but – seventeen-year-old that I was – I was late one more time.

So I peeled a total of 100 kilos.

And I did so without a word, or thought, of complaint.

I've never forgotten Monsieur Hellegouarche. His impressive bearing, the respect he commanded, or those almonds.

I don't use the same punishment in my kitchen. If somebody requires discipline, I'll make them stay late and clean the stove, or something like that.

But I'm never tardy myself, even though I'm running the show, so to speak. If I even begin to suspect that I might get to the restaurant later than I'm expected, I feel a tingling sensation in my thumb and forefinger, and pick up the pace as thoughts of peeling almonds come freshly to mind all over again.

————————

What do you eat for breakfast?
Cereal and espresso coffee.

What dish would you cook in order to seduce someone?
Seafood platter, no cooking, more time to seduce.

What do you never cook?
Processed, convenience or microwave food.

What's the one dish you find hard to get right?
Anything Thai.

On Second Thoughts
TOM AIKENS

*Tom Aikens was born in Norwich in 1970 and grew up in a food-
and wine-loving family. After studying at Norwich City College
Hotel School, he went to work at Mirabelle in Eastbourne, then
came to London to work at two Michelin-starred restaurants:
Cavalier's and the Capital Hotel. He then went to work for chef
Pierre Koffman at La Tante Claire, and in 1993 became sous-chef
at Pied à Terre. In 1996, following time in France working for Joël
Rubuchon and Gerard Boyer, he returned to London to become
head chef and co-proprietor of Pied à Terre where, at twenty-six, he
became the youngest ever recipient of two Michelin stars. In 2003,
Aikens realised his dream of opening his own restaurant when he
and his then wife, Laura, launched Tom Aikens Restaurant in
Chelsea, where he earned a Michelin star in 2004, as well as other
awards and accolades.*

W HEN I WAS asked to contribute to this collection, I
racked my brain for a week, but came up empty. This is

not to suggest that I've never caused, witnessed, or been party to catastrophes in a kitchen. I certainly have. But in time you arrive at a point where you don't make any more mistakes – at least that's the hope, and I've been at that point long enough to have forgotten any disasters I might have made early in my career.

So I was all set to decline the invitation to be part of this anthology when it occurred to me that the biggest error I ever made in the kitchen had nothing to do with mistaking salt for sugar, letting a soufflé collapse, or setting some bit of food on fire. No, the worst catastrophe was one I inflicted on *myself*, the day I basically chucked my whole career. I'll never forget that moment, or the act of kindness that brought me back.

I wasn't even twenty years old when I first came to London to work for David Cavalier at his restaurant, Cavalier's.

I knew that I wanted to be a chef. I've always loved to cook, and decided that's what I wanted to do for a living. But I had very limited experience, having left college a year earlier to work in a restaurant in Eastbourne that, while it had three rosettes in the AA guide, lacked the Michelin cachet of David's one-star place.

I needed the wisdom and worldliness of a place like Cavalier's, so I came to London. I decided to share a flat in Clapham with my twin brother, Robert, who was a chef. To help offset the rent, the two of us rented a room to my cousin, Marguerite Krikhaar, who was a model.

London didn't have the restaurant scene then that it does today. David was one of the few, along with giants such as the Roux brothers, Marco Pierre White, and Pierre Koffman, who could boast even one Michelin star. Because jobs at these chefs' restaurants were in such short supply, they could ask a young cook like me to work for free, and that's what I did, agreeing to three months unpaid, in the hope that a paid job might open up before too long.

The kitchen at Cavalier's was tight, about 3 metres square, with six of us crammed in there cooking together. Days were long: I'd get to work at six in the morning and keep going right through until one o'clock in the morning.

It wasn't a lot of fun: not only were the hours endless, but the workload was overwhelming, and David could be the typical abusive chef, not interested in your problems or excuses for anything that fell short of perfection. All he wanted was excellence in everything you did.

Nonetheless, he was a man of his word, and when a job came up, David offered it to me. I found myself working the vegetable station and making a wage – a small wage, but a wage none-theless.

I was on my way to the career I wanted, and I should have been happy, but there was one factor that was destined to undo me. Every night, after close to twenty hours of gruelling and often degrading work, I'd get home and be greeted by the same scene: Robert, who worked much more regular hours, Mar-guerite and a few of their beautiful friends just returning from an evening that couldn't have been more different from mine, still glowing with the magic of whatever club or restaurant (or both) they had just left, winding down their night on the town, and filling our home with laughter, cigarette smoke, and other signs of great good times.

It was a daily reminder of what I was missing by devoting my whole being to a life in the kitchen.

After one such encounter, I just couldn't take it any more.

This is ridiculous, I thought. I should be having that kind of fun at my age.

Just like that, I decided to give up my job at Cavalier's.

Because I had to be at the restaurant by 6 a.m. every day, I had a set of keys. The next morning, I arrived earlier than usual, like a cat burglar, slipping in at five-thirty. I scribbled a note to David, telling him that I couldn't take it any more, left it for him to discover on a table in the kitchen, hid the key under the mat outside the front door, and went home to get some sleep.

I had no idea what I would do for the rest of my life, but I *did* know what I'd do for the rest of that week: party, *hard*, with Robert, Marguerite, and all her lovely young friends.

And that I did, clubbing until dawn and loving every minute of it.

And then, the most amazing thing happened: a few days later, the phone rang.

It was David Cavalier.

'What's up?' he said to me, sounding much more humane and concerned than I could have imagined, having only known him in the confines of the kitchen where, to be honest, his nightly abuses were one of the things that made me want to get out.

'Why did you leave like that? Why didn't you come to see me?' he went on, still sounding remarkably calm and solicitous, like an understanding father, or older brother.

'Dunno,' I said. And I didn't. I was tired, I was twenty, and I was confused.

He invited me to come over to the restaurant and I did. He sat me down and asked me again why I left.

'It was too hard,' I said.

'Of course it was hard,' he replied matter-of-factly.

'Listen,' he went on. 'If you want to get anywhere in life you have to work your arse off and take a bit of shit and just get on with it.'

I considered this.

Then he *really* floored me.

'I can see you have something in you, Tom. You may be young, but it's clear you have talent. I think you could go places. You'd be silly to chuck it all away.'

When somebody reaches out to you like that, especially when that somebody is one of the best chefs in London, you don't make the same mistake again. You ask them if they'll have you back. I did, and he did.

I stayed on at Cavalier's for just over a year, then got on to the next job, and the next. I have my own place now, and I still love cooking.

I'll always be grateful to David Cavalier for that phone call, and the meeting that followed. I had made what could have been a life-altering mistake, and he corrected it for me, letting me come back to his professional home and continue to grow there.

In life, I suppose, as in kitchens – if you have the right people around you, no catastrophe is irredeemable.

What do you eat for breakfast?
A bowl of porridge, fresh juice of some sort and maybe some eggs – omelette or scrambled on toast.

What dish would you cook in order to seduce someone?
A nice home roast or something simple! There is no point, I feel,

in going for caviar/lobster/foie gras. That's just too obvious. A home-made lasagna is to me amazing just as much as lobster. You make your fresh pasta, a great sauce seasoned just right and a great béchamel with Parmesan.

What do you never cook?
Anything that is endangered. I never cook something just to be different. That's pretentious crap.

What's the one dish you find hard to get right?
I don't think that exists as yet. I make it my priority to master things I'm not good at.

Lost and Found
RAYMOND BLANC

Born in Besançon, France, in 1949, Raymond Blanc opened his first restaurant at the age of twenty-eight. After just one year, it was named Egon Ronay Restaurant of the Year. A Michelin star followed the year after that, and a second star two years later. In 1984, Blanc created the hotel and restaurant Le Manoir aux Quat' Saisons in Great Milton, Oxford, the only country-house hotel in Britain to achieve and sustain two Michelin stars and the Relais and Chateaux Purple Shield. Le Manoir aux Quat' Saisons is further distinguished by its extensive organic herb and vegetable garden. In 1991, Blanc established L'École de Cuisine at Le Manoir, welcoming both enthusiastic amateurs and professional cooks to the kitchen, and in 1996 he opened the first of four Le Petit Blanc brasseries, which went on to receive the Michelin Bib Gourmand. Blanc appears regularly on television and is a member of Slow Food and the Soil Association. He has written many best-sellers, including Cooking for Friends, A Blanc Christmas, Recipes from Le Manoir aux Quat' Saisons, Blanc Vite, *and* Foolproof French Cookery.

EVERYBODY, I SUPPOSE, has a philosophy, and this is mine: there's nothing sadder in life than not finding your talent, something that you're good at and that makes you happy.

It took me a long time to find mine, even though with hindsight it was there from the beginning. As a child, I was very much involved in food. You could say that I served my chef's apprenticeship in my mother's kitchen and my father's garden, usually while my friends were playing football.

In the hierarchy of our home, I was always the minion: if my father went fishing, he'd toss me the fish to clean and scale. If my mother was going to prepare, say, some beans, then I would have to top and tail them, and then she would apply her cooking craft.

When I think back on my childhood, I remember the joy of the dinner table, and the connection to the seasons that my parents' love of food imparted to me, and which in time became the cornerstone of both my philosophy and my cooking.

Yet, strangely enough, it took me years before I truly connected with cooking. My first career decision was made for me by my teachers, who decided I should become an engineer. I hated everything about it. I had no logic, and I hated squares and rectangles.

I decided to set out on a quest for my own little talent. To that end, I took a lot of jobs. I worked as a clothes cutter but found it unsatisfying. Then I became a nurse and seriously contemplated becoming the next Mother Teresa, but this also turned out to be a great failure. I thought I'd be good at drawing, so briefly studied the *beaux arts*, discovering that I wasn't as good as I thought I'd be.

But the most dehumanising job, and the worst experience,

was as a factory worker, a cog in a big impersonal machine. A shadow.

During these years, I was lost, at sea, and scared by the prospect of being unrewarded and mediocre.

Then I had that moment when lightning strikes and you see for the first time what you want to do. It happened unexpectedly, as I was strolling past a restaurant called Le Palais de la Bière in Besançon.

I still remember the scene vividly. It was a perfect summer evening, and in Place Victor Hugo one of the most beautiful scenes was unfolding. On the terrace of the restaurant, a flurry of perfect activity: the maître d'hôtel carved a sea bass, while another waiter flambéed crêpes Suzettes, and all around them was the quiet, balletic movement of the other waiters, perfectly attending to guests, and lovers holding hands.

On that night, I decided to become a chef. At last, I had found my calling!

A few days later, I came unannounced to the restaurant and was granted an audience with the chef.

'You must take me,' I told him, my voice full of enthusiasm and exuberance. 'I will be a great chef!'

It all went terribly wrong. You don't tell a chef you want to be a great chef. You tell a chef that you want to learn, that you'll work hard, that you'll make *his* life easier by being a humble and obedient apprentice.

He turned me away unceremoniously. Because I'd found what I wanted to do with my life, it was a terrible anticlimax. But I understood that my mistake was being over-keen.

A few days later, I begged him to see me again and told him all the right things – that I was unformed clay, ready to be moulded by his wise and talented hands into a competent cook, that I would do *anything* – even clean and wash pots – to enter the industry, *anything* that he told me to.

'Now I will listen to you,' he said, nodding his approval. 'I'll give you a job as a cleaner.'

It's funny: all the cleaning of food I did when I was a child put me off cooking. But now here I was cleaning *floors*, and I was happy. I had a sense of purpose: the floors and toilets of this restaurant had never, I'm sure, looked so clean as after I was done with them. They positively sparkled!

I knew that, if I cleaned the floors, then one day they'd let me clean the food, then one day they'd let me cook the food, and then one day I'd be a chef.

Advancement came even more slowly than that. My first promotion was from cleaning the floors to cleaning the wine glasses. I reduced the breakage by half, and the waiters loved me because I gave them the best, most beautiful glasses they had ever used.

I also took every opportunity to learn, no matter how small. Whenever I found myself alone with a glass, even a used one, I'd swirl and sniff the wines, making mental notes of their attributes, remembering the character of each grape variety, looking at the different way different wines' 'legs' ran down the side of the glass, and so on.

Essentially, I was educating myself. Food became my life. I dreamt about food and I had nightmares about food. I read every single book that had to do with food, including those about food science, food chemistry, and so on. My energy was boundless.

My next promotion came a few months later when the restaurant's owner handed me a purple jacket with silver epaulettes and promoted me to *commis débarrasseur*, the lowest category of waiter, only permitted to shuttle food from the kitchen to the dining room and strictly forbidden to interact with the guests.

I hate being patient. But I was also obsessed with food, dreaming about it every night. I just couldn't wait to be a cook, to serve people meals prepared by my own hand.

As an outlet for this burgeoning passion, I began throwing little parties for my friends after my sixteen-hour shifts at work. Two or three times a week, I would have them over to my flat and cook for them – I'd prepare dishes my mother cooked, and started learning to make some of the classics. I remember making my first *beurre blanc*, and roasting a sea bass on fennel and star anise, which nearly bankrupted me!

Just as I had sniffed the glasses when I was a cleaner, I began to taste sauces and other preparations, trying to decipher their complexities, their depth. I felt that I was a part of the restaurant's family by this time, and occasionally I would tell the chef – a giant who was renowned for his terrible temper – that a certain sauce seemed too salty, or too lemony, or too rich. He never responded to my comments, but then, one day, I started telling him my opinion of a certain sauce, I can't remember which one, and his grey eyes got darker and darker. Rage built up within him until he couldn't contain it any longer: he smacked me in the face with a copper pan, knocking out some of my teeth, and stormed off.

Outside the restaurant, as I dabbed at my bloody mouth with a towel, my boss explained the way of the world to me. 'Raymond, I know you mean well, but are you mad? The chef is all: he's the creative force. He makes the place successful. He puts the roof over our heads, buys my car. And you tell him he doesn't know what he's doing. You can't stay here any more. I'll find you a job in England.'

And that's how I ended up in England, in 1972, as a waiter in a restaurant near Witney. The chef was the worst I had ever seen. He hated food: he murdered it, ruined it, and froze it, often weeks in advance, and used other unfathomable short cuts. But I never offered my opinion. Rather, having learnt my lesson at home, I befriended him.

In time, as our 'friendship' evolved, he let me cook some dishes: the proprietor and customers loved them.

One day, the chef and his brigade stormed out, and the owner invited me to take over the kitchen. I accepted the challenge and entered the kitchen basically disguised as a chef, with two English cordon-bleu graduates at my side, and started cooking my heart out.

The adventure had begun. We completely changed the garden, with seed varieties sent by my father. The first harvest was rewarding, and so was the whole first year as the *Michelin Guide* recognised our efforts.

In 1977, at long last, I opened my own restaurant, Les Quat' Saisons in Summertown, Oxford, a tiny place next door to a shop that sold ladies' underwear on one side and Oxfam on the other – nothing to suggest greatness. It was a simple, unassuming restaurant with red-and-white tablecloths and cheap prints on the wall. The building was lined with corrugated iron, so it was freezing in the winter and boiling in the summer, but it was mine and I loved every inch of it.

I couldn't believe what happened next. Within a year, we were named Egon Ronay Restaurant of the Year – the most incredible thing that could happen to a restaurant at that time.

Everything changed! Suddenly, my humble little restaurant

was hosting royalty, including the Queen Mother. I was the toast of the town! The Golden Boy! It was a dream come true.

To show off the new boy, Egon Ronay organised a luncheon at the Dorchester Hotel, where I was to cook for fifty of the top culinary figures of the moment, including many of my heroes, such as the Roux brothers, Anton Mosiman, and Pierre Koffman.

This was an enormous honour for me, and also a great challenge: Les Quat' Saisons only sat thirty guests, and here I was supposed to cook for almost double that number, all of them culinary celebrities – what a frightening thought.

As this afternoon approached, it became clear that what had always been one of the great advantages of my career – the fact that I had never been formally trained – was also a weakness, because I had never been taught one of the basics of the kitchen: to prepare as much food as can be responsibly prepared in advance, without sacrificing quality.

I had never cooked in high-volume restaurants, had never been schooled in the banquet style. For a lunch of this scale and status, a classically trained chef would have prepared dishes that could have simply been finished to order, but I didn't know this.

At one o'clock in the morning, I finished my evening service. We packed up all the raw ingredients, all to be cooked at the Dorchester, which was completely crazy as puff pastry could have been prepared in advance, and so could a lot of the other menu items.

We arrived at the Dorchester at 3 a.m., and cooked right through the night because the menu was so ambitious.

Things that I could usually do without thinking were coming out wrong. For example, I began making puff pastry, and after the fourth turn I could see that it was beginning to weep tears of butter.

My young, inexperienced team were exhausted, and so was I. What had I done wrong? Was the dough too hot? Had I used the wrong type of flour? I never worked out what the problem was but I *willed* the dough to hold together, and I set it aside.

And so it went, all evening and into the morning. By eleven o'clock, our nerves were completely frayed.

The event began and, after a short reception at twelve noon, we sent out the first course: scallops in puff pastry. Each guest was waiting for that special moment and taste. I put the little dishes in the oven, and soon they began to leak all over the place. Instead of a flaky, melting and even pastry, a rough-puff pastry appeared.

I had no choice: I sent it out. At that moment, I felt sick. That day my professional pride was tested to the limit.

Next up were the pâtés of turbot, which were cooked in two different ovens. Having tested one oven, I assumed that the other oven's temperature would be fine. But it was not: when I carved the first slice of the fluffy, light, heavenly-smelling pâté, I managed a slight smile, but it was soon lost as the second lot of pâtés came out of the other oven barely cooked . . . some of these very famous chefs found themselves eating raw and cold pâté. My five-year-old reputation, so dearly acquired, was ruined in just a few minutes . . .

I still had three courses to go and I was already devastated. I wanted so much to make the most beautiful food for these people. Not to show off, mind you, but to please them, the way they had pleased me in their restaurants, or their cookbooks, or both.

I managed to get through the next two courses and, miraculously, the final course, my caramel soufflé, came out just right, at the moment I was about to take my large, very sharp knife and commit hara-kiri.

This was the most humbling professional experience of my life, and certainly the worst meal I had ever cooked. Worse than any meal I had ever prepared for my family. Worse than any meal I had prepared for my friends in the middle of the night, after work back in Besançon. Worse than anything any young cook in my kitchen had ever put before me.

Of course it was! Because I was trying to do the impossible.

I felt I let down everyone that day – my mother, the poor guys working with me, the great chefs who had taken time out to come and see who this new kid was and what all the fuss was about.

I had lost face. But all of the guys were very nice to me. When I came into the dining room, they could not have been more sympathetic or understanding. They applauded, sincerely. I could see in their eyes, though, that they felt bad for me, a little embarrassed. The caramel soufflé wasn't good enough to have made them forget the rest of the meal.

'What kind of ending is *that*?' you may wonder. Poor Raymond Blanc, standing there with the great chefs of London heaping polite applause upon him. That's a terrible ending.

But that isn't the ending, of course. All of those chefs, every one of them, visited me at my restaurant before too long. And when they did, I cooked them the meal I knew I could, the kind of meal I had wanted to make for them at the Dorchester.

And the real ending, you see, hasn't even taken place yet. I'm still learning about food, about people, about how to create special moments for them. This year, we celebrated our twenty-first anniversary, and I still never look back, always keeping my eyes forward, on what's next. I hope the story won't be over for many, many years.

And, yet, if you look at it another way, the ending – the true and happy ending – took place well *before* the lunch. Before Egon Ronay honoured me with the award. The ending, for me, occurred when I became a chef, and while that afternoon at the Dorchester was not my finest moment – in fact, it was my worst – I never for a second doubted my calling.

I became a chef, you see. I had found my little talent, even though I managed to misplace it for a few hours. I had avoided the tragedy of not discovering what I wanted to do with my life. What happier ending could there be than that?

What do you eat for breakfast?
It varies occasionally, but most days I have coffee, brown toast and fresh carrot juice, and at weekends I treat myself to a cooked breakfast.

What dish would you cook in order to seduce someone?
Finger food, of course; that can be oysters, beautiful big pink prawns and then something with chocolate is a definite.

What do you never cook?
Beefburgers.

What's the one dish you find hard to get right?
Grilled insects (only joking). Probably a terrine.

The 'No Choice' Life
SALLY CLARKE

After gaining a diploma in hotel and catering at Croydon Technical College, Sally Clarke studied at Le Cordon Bleu School in Paris. She then spent four years in California, where she met her friend and mentor, Alice Waters of Chez Panisse in Berkeley. In 1983, she returned to London and the following year opened Clarke's Restaurant in Kensington Church Street. In 1998, she opened the shop & Clarke's, selling freshly baked breads, pastries and high-quality ingredients used in the restaurant. In 2000, she launched her Clarke's Bread, which now produces up to 2,000 loaves a night and sells to many central London restaurants, hotels, caterers, and shops. She is the author of Sally Clarke's Book: Recipes from a Restaurant, Shop and Bakery, *winner of the Glenfiddich award for Food Book of the Year.*

FOR DINNER AT my restaurant, Clarke's, we offer a set, 'no choice' menu that changes nightly. I plan a week's worth of menus in advance – basing them on what's in season, and making decisions founded on the ripeness of fruits and vegetables, the look of salad leaves, and so on – then post them on our website for all to see.

The only time we deviate from the electronically published menu is if for some reason a planned ingredient doesn't make it to our door on the day it's expected, or isn't up to our standards when it arrives, a caveat that's explained, in brief, in a menu footnote. (I handwrite the menus daily, so although it might deviate from what's on our site, the menu is always in sync with the guests' meal.) Of course, we also do what we can to accommodate food allergies.

In many ways, operating like this means always working on a knife's edge. Everything has to be perfect because, for the most part, what we have is what we cook – there's not much extra inventory in the kitchen, so if something goes awry there are precious few alternatives to call on.

This is especially true because we make *everything* fresh from scratch at Clarke's, and most of our food arrives on the day it will be served, so we don't even have the option of poaching from tomorrow's ingredients to solve today's problem, because they simply aren't here yet.

Now it may surprise you to learn that despite the non-existent margin for error, we don't use recipes in my kitchen, except in the pastry department, where *exact* recipes are *de rigueur*. We decide what we'd like to cook and serve, then make things up as we go, by look and feel, which to me is the normal way to cook.

As you might imagine, this approach requires being sur-rounded by a team of like-minded individuals, intuitive cooks who can function this way and who share my sensibility and palate, or at least are able to understand and imitate it. They know, for example, when I ask them to sear a piece of fish with the skin on, how crispy I want that skin, or when I say we're going to make a salad of so-and-so, how I like it seasoned and dressed.

All of this, I believe, keeps things fresh and spontaneous, both in the kitchen and on the plate.

For example, today I was cooking a dish of steamed Scottish mussels, with a little cream sauce drizzled over the top. I couldn't tell you the quantities of each ingredient in the sauce. All I can tell you is what was in it and that I cooked it until the consistency and aroma seemed right, and if I made it tomorrow, it would be more or less the same, but slightly different, owing to my mood tomorrow and perhaps to my evaluation of the way it came out today.

This works fine, 99.9 per cent of the time. But there have been those rare moments when the system has failed, although thankfully the two very worst mishaps occurred about fifteen years ago.

The first took place on the night I had decided to make red-pepper pasta – not a pasta with red-pepper sauce, but rather a pasta with red peppers in the dough.

To make the pasta, we grilled the requisite number of peppers, turning them on the flame until they were nicely blackened. Once cool, we removed and discarded their skins and seeds, puréed the peppers, then worked the purée into the dough, resulting in a beguiling red tint that I was certain would please our guests' eyes, then delight their palates with its smoky sweetness.

As we began to put segments of the dough through the roller, however, the strands that emerged seemed a little soft . . . but I though they'd be fine once they were cooked.

As service started, we began putting the pasta in a large pot of salted, boiling water, portion by portion, as each table approached that course. The red strands sank down into the bubbling water, as pasta will do, but as they floated back up to the surface they didn't look like pasta ribbons at all. Instead, they became a gloopy, soupy, irredeemable mess, and each subsequent attempt produced the same result.

It was so unsuccessful that we couldn't serve it, and I never tried that idea again.

The other disaster that's stayed lodged in my memory for a decade and a half took place shortly after I returned from Venice, where I had enjoyed some lovely grilled white polenta. I decided to try it at Clarke's using the golden polenta that we prefer.

You make polenta in the usual way, stirring cornmeal in water, milk, stock, cream, or some combination thereof until it comes together and attains a porridge-like consistency. You then cool it on a baking sheet, and chill it. As it chills, it hardens, whereupon you can slice it into shapes and sauté it, or in this case lay it across the grates of a grill.

Like that red-pepper pasta, the polenta in the pot seemed a bit wet to me, although it firmed up when chilled, and we were able to slice it. Once we set it on the grill, however, we learnt almost immediately that it was indeed too runny. As it warmed up, rather than sit there like a nice crisp lump with beautiful bar marks, it began to drip through the grates and catch fire on the coals.

As unfortunate as those stories are, I must say that they weren't completely useless affairs. One learns every day and as you move through the years you see things better than when you were younger. These were growing experiences, to be sure, and they contributed to my ability to discern looming disasters, which I didn't have before the pasta disintegrated, before the polenta melted into the smouldering coals.

They made me a more careful cook, more attuned to the potential for problems, and less likely to disregard what that little warning bell at the back of my mind was trying to tell me when I thought that the pasta dough and the polenta were too soft.

And despite these moments, I can't think of another way I'd be happy working. I simply don't believe that I could bear the drudgery of executing a menu that only changed four times a year.

No matter how much I learn, though, I'm quite certain there will always be stresses and strains. I think that challenges like these are what keep most people motivated. If you haven't got anything to worry about in life, you become a bored and boring person.

Like this very afternoon, I was expecting fourteen lamb loins for dinner, but the butcher only sent me four, and I need to finish here and go and decide what to do.

I don't know quite how I'll solve it, but I'm looking forward to working it out with my team and to serving the delicious solution to our guests in a few hours.

That's restaurant life for you.

What do you eat for breakfast?
Nothing Monday to Friday; Saturday and Sunday, buttermilk

pancakes, granola, Illy coffee, home-made English muffins with apricot-kernel jam – all from Clarke's.

What dish would you cook in order to seduce someone?
Find me someone to seduce and I'll work it out.

What do you never cook?
Turkey Twizzlers and spaghetti hoops.

What's the one dish you find hard to get right?
Toast.

The Boiling Point
ROWLEY LEIGH

After a variety of schools, Cambridge, a spell of dairy farming and a misspent youth in the snooker halls of Fulham, Rowley Leigh got a job at the Joe Allen restaurant in Covent Garden as a grill and short-order chef. He migrated to Le Gavroche and learnt classical French cooking under the inspired tutelage of Albert Roux before a spell as baker, butcher and buyer to the group. He returned to the kitchen as sous-chef and then head chef of Le Poulbot in the City of London before opening the trailblazing Kensington Place in Notting Hill with Nick Smallwood and Simon Slater in 1987. He is still there, and is a director of Moving Image Restaurants. He is food correspondent of the Financial Times, *after a spell with the* Guardian *and the* Sunday Telegraph, *and has won two Glenfiddich awards for the quality of his newspaper writing. His book,* No Place Like Home, *was shortlisted for the André Simon Award and won the Jeremy Round prize from the Guild of Food Writers. He has three children and lives with his wife Kate in Shepherd's Bush.*

THIS IS THE story of what was, by far, the most extreme, brutal, frightening thing that has ever happened in my kitchen. I've never heard of it happening in another kitchen, but I'm quite certain that similar incidents must have occurred elsewhere, because there are knives everywhere in kitchens, and it's hot, and kitchens are populated by people who don't always see eye to eye.

But then again, I've been in this business for a long time, and it's the only such incident I know of, so perhaps I am the lone chef-restaurateur unfortunate enough to have had it happen in his place of business.

In any event, it took place in 1992 in my restaurant Kensington Place, and involves three primary *dramatis personae*. The first, a slightly twisted, extremely competent cook, we'll call Malcolm. Though not an elder *per se*, Malcolm was one of the more seasoned members of my kitchen brigade, and he was old school, both in his technique and in his penchant for treating underlings rudely. If the truth be told, I was always rather worried about him inspiring exactly the kind of story you're about to hear.

Then there was an Aussie guy we'll call Pat, who had been with me for about a year. He was as sweet and charming and dedicated as anyone you could have hoped to have on your team. A hard worker, with a smile for everyone and always eager to help out, he was a delight in every way, truly the perfect employee. The third player is the catalyst of the action, a young apprentice named, for our purposes, Dwight.

From the day he arrived on the scene, Dwight struck me as rather odd. I wouldn't have deemed him schizophrenic exactly, but he seemed to be almost in conflict with himself – he was both very quiet and very intense, and though he was clearly serious about his work, that seriousness always seemed to come with great effort, as though he were straining to maintain his attention or composure.

I'll put it more succinctly: Dwight was a bit creepy.

He gave you the feeling that there was something simmering just beneath the surface. His demeanour was like a vibrating lid on top of a pot of violently boiling water, and there was a constant sense that it would only take a few more degrees for the lid to come flying off.

Now, there are personal dynamics in any kitchen. Sometimes, especially in smaller restaurants, there's total and complete harmony. But the more people you have on board, the more potential there is for tension.

Our staff had about twenty-five people on it, and so some conflict was inevitable, especially with the likes of Malcolm and Dwight in the mix.

One day, after Dwight had been with us for about a month, word travelled to my office that he and the surly Malcolm had had an altercation in the kitchen.

The story came to me second hand, so I can't relate all the specifics, but the long and short of it is that the incident was punctuated by Dwight's throwing a plate at Malcolm.

This is one of those things that you simply cannot condone in a kitchen. Violent behaviour in any workplace is unacceptable, but in a business of this nature – where there are hot stoves near by and bladed objects everywhere, and customers on the other side of the swinging doors trying to enjoy a meal in comfort – then there must be a policy of zero tolerance.

So I gave Malcolm a warning for his participation in the altercation, and sacked young Dwight for perpetuating the actual violence. Dwight took the news with barely a word, nodding his understanding, and leaving the premises with a serenity that, in hindsight, I find haunting.

We went about the rest of our day, closed the restaurant that night, and reopened the following morning.

At about 10 a.m., I was working in my office when a shadow fell across my desk. I looked up, and was startled to see Dwight standing there.

'It's perfectly all right,' he assured me, explaining that he understood why I had had to let him go. As always there was that sense of an internal tug-of-war, but he did seem to have himself firmly in tow.

'Do you mind if I go and pick up my knives and other possessions in the kitchen?' he asked.

'That's fine,' I said. We shook hands, and I went about my work.

I had a sous-chef in those days – we'll call her Nancy – and Nancy came from a pretty rough area, so nothing really fazed her. But something had transpired that she thought merited my attention, and so she had come up to see me, appearing in the doorway mere minutes after Dwight had said goodbye.

'Chef,' she said to me in her matter-of-fact way, 'I think you'd better come down to the kitchen. Dwight has gone berserk and is stabbing everybody.'

She was so calm that it took me a moment to realise the true meaning of her words, but as I played them back four of them sank in – *Dwight, Berserk, Stabbing, Everybody.*

I leapt from my desk, pushed past Nancy, and ran to the kitchen to find that three of my strongest and most reliable kitchen porters had the struggling Dwight in a headlock. He had finally bubbled over, you see, and, once unleashed, his fury was such that it took all three of them to restrain him.

It was instantly apparent that I had missed the violence by mere seconds; in fact, Malcolm and Pat were still reeling.

Here's what had happened as I later pieced it together: Dwight left my office and went to the kitchen, as I'd given him permission to do. He picked up his knives and started to leave, whereupon Malcolm decided to try and stop him.

The two men began to taunt one another, Dwight trying to sidestep Malcolm, and Malcolm repositioning himself in his path. As tempers mounted, Dwight changed his grip on his chef's knife, getting it into a position from which he could stab somebody.

Seeing this, Pat – the earnest young Aussie – stepped in, whereupon Dwight, meaning to stab Malcolm, plunged the knife down between Pat's shoulder blades, landing it on the collar bone. Dwight removed the blade, then turned for Malcolm, who by this time was trying to get away, and when Dwight swung again all he was able to manage was a minor cut on Malcolm's hand. This was when a few of the other guys pounced on Dwight and got him under control, and Nancy came looking for me.

Once Dwight simmered down, I sought to diffuse the situation by instructing my cooks to release him. It was silly of me, I suppose, but they were manhandling him in a very rough fashion, and he clearly had expended his energy, and his anger, and I thought it best for everyone if he left. No sooner was he let go than he bolted out of the restaurant and took off running down the street and out of sight.

I'm not certain how the events of the morning were explained to the Emergency Services operator, but within half an hour there must have been twenty-five people in the restaurant. We had become a fully fledged crime scene, with police asking for statements, paramedics running to and fro with stretchers and the like, and doctors in white coats ready to attend to the wounded. It was mayhem, to say the least, and it became surreal when a police helicopter swooped down and landed in the school playground next door.

Before too long, the wounded were carted off to hospital and, with some time to reflect, I found myself in a state of shock and more than a little traumatised, because I felt responsible, even though Dwight was clearly a psychopath. Nonetheless, it had happened in my restaurant, on my patch, and I felt terrible about it.

Now, here's the thing: being in the restaurant business, we had a classic 'show must go on' frame of mind, even after a morning like that. So once the police cars, ambulances and helicopter had gone, we cleaned the place up and opened for lunch, and did so right on time.

While my staff served our guests, I shot round to the hospital and saw the boys. Malcolm was discharged immediately, though in his typically disgruntled fashion he complained like hell that he was much too ill to come back to work.

Pat, on the other hand, the hero of the story, was off work for about a month, so severe was his injury. He returned, still with that smile on his face, and ready to work as hard as before, insisting that he receive no special treatment whatsoever.

And what of the knife-wielding Dwight? He was caught later the afternoon of the stabbings, and arrested. Not surprisingly he was found by the experts to be mentally disturbed, and certifiably so. But there seemed to be a good soul somewhere inside him, though it was clearly losing that internal struggle that suddenly made so much sense.

In the end, Dwight impressed me, because he had clear remorse for what he had done, and wanted to be sentenced immediately, even against the advice of his lawyer, with whom he argued in court. Dwight didn't want to be psychologically assessed; he wanted to be punished. I respected that, and appreciated it, and this may surprise you, but I attended his trial and spoke up for him.

Oddly, the fellow I look back on with most disdain was Malcolm, whom I tried my best to make comfortable when he returned to work, despite his endless grousing, and who then went on to leave my employ and spout unsavoury remarks about me to the worst, most shit-staining food columnist in the country.

So what have we learnt from this tale of violence in the kitchen? Is there a moral to this story?

I suppose there is, and it applies to cooking as much as it does to people. When you see a lid vibrating ever more violently on top of a pot, or sense the smell of burning food in the air, or simply have a notion that something's *wrong* or about to go wrong – don't ignore the signs, or your instincts: get the situation under control before things boil over.

(*As told to Andrew Friedman.*)

What do you eat for breakfast?
When not working: toast, bacon and marmalade, or kippers, if available. When working I nibble at the staff lunch at eleven-thirty.

What dish would you cook in order to seduce someone?
Scrambled eggs with truffles or caviar or sea-urchin roe.

What do you never cook?
Okra. Domestic pets. Steak tartare.

What's the one dish you find hard to get right?
The last one.

Man's Best Friend
ANTONIO CARLUCCIO

Antonio Carluccio was born in the south of Italy and raised in the north. He lived in Austria and Germany, and worked as a journalist and wine merchant before moving to London in 1975. In the early 1980s, he managed the Neal Street Restaurant in Covent Garden, which he now owns with his wife, Priscilla. He has starred in two BBC TV cooking series, and written a dozen books, including Carluccio's Complete Italian Food, Antonio Carluccio Goes Wild, Antonio Carluccio's Italian Feast, *and* Italia. *Together with his wife he is the owner of and inspiration behind Carluccio's Caffés, a successful combination of food shop, deli, and restaurant.*

F OR THIRTEEN YEARS, I had the most wonderful companion a man could ask for, my trusty dog, Jan.

Jan was a Berger de Picardie shepherd, similar to a German shepherd dog, but much, much nicer, and with longer hair that I found quite distinguished. Jan had a face so warm it could melt ice. He was always with me. We were so close that I even dedicated one of my books to him – if you open a copy of *The Complete Mushroom Book: The Quiet Hunt*, you'll see a picture of him there at the front.

I put him there not because he had a gift for sniffing out mushrooms, but because he was often with me in the woods when I'd go foraging, and I'd find him rolling among the mushrooms in the grass, having found them by sheer luck.

I always thought of Jan more as a friend than a canine. And we had many moments that I remember the way you might remember moments when a friend did something unthinkable and hysterical. For instance, one day, we were walking in Hyde Park. We came across a little dog, a chihuahua, I think, with a diamond lead and a pink bow. Well, Jan thought this was just too ridiculous and precious, so he lifted his leg and showered the little thing with a big pee. Within seconds, the other dog was shaking and wet, as though it had just come in from the rain. Its owner, a similarly overdressed woman, screamed in horror.

I apologised politely, of course, but the truth is that I found it rather funny. For years, I'd often remember that moment and have a laugh about it.

As a cook, I'm very particular, not only about what I eat, but also about what I feed to those I love. Since I loved Jan more than anyone else in the world then, I *never* fed him dog food. Instead, he would eat whatever I ate. If I roasted myself a chicken, then I'd cut him some chicken. If it was vegetables, then he'd have vegetables. Like a loyal spouse, he always let me know he loved my food by eating every last crumb, even though I often gave him the bits and pieces that I burnt.

I got Jan in Ibiza and brought him with me to Germany. When we moved to England in 1975, he had to be quarantined for six months, according to the law. I wasn't pleased, and neither was he; he was about 100 miles from London, where I was, and for a dog six months is a lifetime, especially when he's used to home cooking.

I was always very proud of the fact that I never fed dear Jan dog food, but I must confess that his being accustomed to people food did lead to some unfortunate incidents. Because he had never been trained to steer clear of the dinner table – indeed, he was often my only companion there in those early days – he thought it perfectly acceptable to help himself to whatever food *other* people might be eating, or expecting to eat.

For example, I'm lucky to be successful now, but when I was younger, and living in Hamburg, I had my own business as a wine merchant, and business wasn't very good. Consequently, I had very little money. Craving steak one day, I splurged and bought myself a steak, even though I shouldn't have.

All afternoon I thought of that steak and how good it would be after I seasoned it, seared it in the pan, finished it in the oven, and drizzled it with olive oil. I was consumed with the anticipation of that moment when I would cut into it and see the juicy, red, rare grain of the meat within.

That night, I cooked it, the smell and sizzle filling my senses and increasing my already substantial appetite. I set the steak on a plate, turned round to find a piece of bread, and turned back just in time to see Jan yank the steak off the table with his teeth, and scamper down the hall.

I hurried after him, but by then it was too late. He had devoured the whole thing.

I was so broke that I sat down and cried. Not just because that steak was lost, but also because I couldn't afford another one. (I subsequently learnt that steak was Jan's favourite food.)

Then there was the time I was enlisted to prepare all the food for a lavish cocktail party for some very special friends. I spent the whole morning cooking in my home, making little canapés, lining metal trays with them, and covering them with aluminium foil. Because I worked alone, I could only transport two trays to the car at a time. On returning from storing the first load, I discovered that the rest of my canapés had disappeared into the mouth of my beloved dog.

That was the one time I was angry with him in all our years together.

I stayed angry for three days. When I finally got over it and began showing him affection again, he took me back with open paws, licking my face as if nothing had happened.

Dogs are like that. No matter how mean you are to them – and, after all, it was my fault he ate the canapés because I never trained him to know better – when you're ready to be sweet, they're there waiting for you.

One terrible day, Jan disappeared. I couldn't find him anywhere and I was beside myself. He was gone for a month, but I never gave up hope.

I missed him so badly that I convinced somebody at the newspaper, the London *Evening Standard*, to write a story about him, complete with a photograph. The day after the story ran, I got a call from somebody from the East End, but it turned out to be a scam, someone who wanted to extort money from me. Then I had a call from a man in Wembley telling me that he had seen the article and recently taken in a dog who looked just like the one in the paper. It seemed impossible, because Wembley was quite a distance away, but I asked them to hold the phone up to the dog's ear. They did, and I whistled. They reported that he recognised my whistle, wagging his tail and licking the phone.

I drove up to Wembley and, sure enough, there was Jan. He must have walked for two or three days to get there, and one of his paws was sore, so I had to take special care of him. But I had him back, and I couldn't have been happier.

With the exception of that month, and the time he was in quarantine, Jan was always by my side, and there was always some mishap concerning food. For instance, when I first met my wife, Priscilla, she had her own children. We went to visit them at Bryanston School in Dorset, and the dog was with us. The focal point of the day was a big picnic in the grounds of the school, a very civilised affair during which each family set up its own blanket and sat on the grass sharing a meal in the company of other pupils' families.

It was a lovely, pastoral scene, but everyone there must have been a bit surprised when they saw my friend Jan strolling from blanket to blanket on all fours, quietly stealing food from everybody in his path. You miserable hound, I thought. Eventually, I put a lead on him and apologised to the other families. But, like that time he showered that silly little dog in Hyde Park, I secretly thought it was hysterical.

Friends seem to get each other, and that's why Jan was so dear to me. I let him be himself and he let me be myself, and the two of us got along wonderfully. We were so close that, one Christmas, I made Jan a painting of a Christmas tree, with sausages hanging off its branches like ornaments. I'm sure he didn't understand what it was, and if he did, that it did nothing to discourage his love of people food.

But that's all right. In fact, I wouldn't have had it any other way.

What do you eat for breakfast?
I recently discovered porridge, which is very healthy and helps the body.

What dish would you cook in order to seduce someone?
I think everyone would succumb to this dish: freshly made tagliolini – ideally your loved one should be watching as you make them – served with a simple tomato sauce and basil, as you won't have much time for preparation. Slurp the tagliolini just like in *The Lady and the Tramp*.

What do you never cook?
Indian food, as I find it very challenging to combine the perfect quality and quantity of spices.

What's the one dish you find hard to get right?
Soufflé, but my wife Priscilla makes a perfect one.

A Walk on the Moon
SHAUN HILL

Born in London, Shaun Hill garnered his early cooking experience at such restaurants as Carrier's in Islington, the Gay Hussar in Soho, and the Intercontinental Hotel on Hyde Park Corner. He was chef of Gidleigh Park from 1985 to 1994 and then of his own restaurant, Merchant House, Ludlow, from 1994 to 2005, during which time it won one Michelin star and three rosettes from the AA. Among his many accolades, Hill was named The Egon Ronay Guide's *Chef of the Year in 1993 and the same year won the Caterer and Hotelkeeper Chef award. Hill is a research fellow at Exeter University's Department of Classics, menu consultant to British Airways, and the author of many books, including* The Cook's Book, Food in Ancient Times, *and* Cooking at the Merchant House.*

M Y RESTAURANT, Merchant House, was tiny. It comprised half the ground floor of a fifteenth-century building in a small medieval town on the Welsh border. I bought it because I didn't need to ask the bank for any money to open such a small place. I got planning permission and launched with what was basically a domestic kitchen with a bit of commercial equipment, and enough seats for twenty-four people.

Instead of having a kitchen brigade – a team of assistant chefs and line cooks – I elected to toil alone in the confines of this space, with my wife helping me, and a waitress to serve the food.

At the time I committed to this humble existence, I had a reasonably good reputation, and many of my colleagues and industry observers considered it a sort of madness as a career move. But it worked fine. We did well right up until we closed the restaurant at the end of February 2005. We were handed a Michelin star from day one, and got top ratings in all the right food guides, and all the other sorts of things that help make a restaurant successful.

But life at Merchant House wasn't without its challenges. The first, and in some ways, highest hurdle to clear was our plan to have this ancient structure double as our home. When I applied for planning permission to use part of the ground floor as a restaurant, the inspector of buildings came round to determine what changes had to be made. He surveyed the first floor, where our bedroom is, then thanked us for our time and departed.

The next day, the inspector returned, seemingly in a state of panic, and told us that he hadn't been able to sleep that night for fear that our windows weren't big enough for us to escape if there was a fire. The windows of course had been like that since Cromwell and nobody had been killed as yet, but none of that mattered to the inspector, who of course had the power to stop our plan dead in its tracks.

This problem had a surprisingly simple resolution: some-where along the way the inspector let on that it would be all right if that room wasn't the bedroom. So we renamed it the *lobby* . . . and we have slept in the lobby ever since.

That, in a nutshell, is bureaucracy for you.

It's also a good example of the fact that when you live, or cook, in a building that dates back to 1430, you have to make all kinds of concessions. Accordingly, the menu for Merchant House was developed around the difficulties of the place, which really was not meant to be knocked around to comply with regulations. So fitting bits and pieces of equipment into the kitchen was more of a job than it would normally be. The kitchen was so cramped that I would only have espresso when the restaurant was closed, because I had no room for a machine in there. But I was able to fashion a reasonable, functioning professional home. We had the essentials: an oven, a stove with the requisite number of burners, a pot sink, and so on.

As time went on, I'd add little touches to make myself as comfortable as possible. For example, although there is no music in the dining room, I used to listen to Mozart in the kitchen because it made the place seem more tranquil. (In truth, it also provided a noise barrier, so that when guests informed the waitress that they were allergic to three-quarters of the menu, they couldn't hear me kicking the door in frustration.)

Because of the limitations of the kitchen, my entire system of cooking was founded on an extreme sort of organisation. Things were so compulsively arranged that a blind man could go in the fridge and find things exactly where they'd been a year before. Things had to be like this, or I wouldn't have had room to store all the goods we kept.

The same was true during lunch and dinner service. I had nowhere to keep my finished food hot, so I would cook everything in the right order, and with the right timing, so that all the dishes for one table were finished at the same time.

I was able to do this nightly, even though I'd bring all the vegetables, even the potatoes, up from the raw state, cooking them to order. I had a highly idiosyncratic system of woks with stock or water in them, and my eyes and ears in ten places at once. The whole thing hung together on a series of intricate and small timings, and required intense and unrelenting concentration. By the end of each night, I was exhausted, but pulling this kind of thing off every twenty-four hours was also a source of tremendous pride.

There was just one problem: I have a particular taste for Welsh rarebit – the toasted Cheddar cheese sandwiches which are classically cooked in a salamander, an open-sided grill, able to produce incredibly high heat. I like my cheese mixed with mustard and Worcester sauce, but that hardly mattered, because the one thing that I didn't have room for in this kitchen was a salamander.

After about six years, I felt I deserved my toasted cheese, and I began to devise a plan whereby I could fit a salamander into the tiny kitchen.

Wouldn't that be something, I thought to myself. *Not only to have my favourite thing, but also to be able to serve grilled red mullet and skin-on fish and other high-heat preparations to the guests.*

I became obsessed, furtively looking around the kitchen whenever I had the time, and trying to imagine where I would put the salamander, where the extractor would go, and how I'd get it all to please the health-and-safety people.

At long last, I identified a place for the salamander, a bit high up, but reachable and serviceable, and perfectly legal.

I had it installed, and for several weeks I had Welsh rarebit for lunch most days and I started to put dishes on the menu that were well suited to grilling.

Because any addition to the kitchen was a rare and significant event, I looked on this salamander as my fourth child, something that would bring inordinate happiness to my life and increase my joy of living.

Although the machine was at a manageable height, because of its unusual positioning, there were certain things one could not properly observe, and after it had been in for about three weeks, a substantial amount of oil had built up on its cooking surface.

When did I finally learn this important bit of information?

It was eight-fifteen on a Saturday night, the most fraught time in most kitchens' weeks, because this is the one night that everybody eats out and they all want to have their dinner at about eight o'clock. This was also a time when there was a great deal of interest in the restaurant, so on any given night there were at least two food writers in the house, and sometimes more of them than anyone else.

Sure enough, during this peak frenzy, I looked up from the stove to find that the red mullet in the salamander had caught fire. Indeed, they no longer resembled food, having become, essentially, charcoal. Now this wasn't a great big fire, but fires do require extinguishing, so I picked up the extinguisher. I had never used an extinguisher before, although all chefs have them in their kitchens.

I put what seemed like a pressure commensurate with the situation at hand on the trigger, which is to say hardly any pressure at all.

It turns out that this was one of those extinguishers that put out fires with a smothering powder, and the little steel canister spewed out enough of it to coat everything in the kitchen, including the just-completed dinner for four that was all set to go out. The dust got in the prepared sauces, on all the dinner plates, on my cutting board, on the floor. Everywhere.

We have a credo in the restaurant business, our equivalent of 'The show must go on': 'The food must be served.'

This was especially apt at my restaurant because we had a three- to four-month waiting list for years, with people booking months in advance. So there was nobody there who'd simply been hungry that night and wandered in; these were all people for whom dinner at Merchant House was a special occasion, which made it difficult to wander through and say, 'It's all gone wrong, I'm going to the pub,' which, to be honest, is what I felt like doing more than anything else in the world.

As for that white powder, I had no clue whether it was poisonous or not, so the only thing to do was bin all the food, clean all the plates, and start from scratch.

I quickly closed the kitchen door, turned up my Mozart, and set about reversing the situation. My first task was to clean every plate and bowl, and wipe clean my work surface. It occurred to me, even at that moment, that this disaster reflected the essential ridiculousness of restaurants, which is that you do things that are difficult while attempting to give an appearance that it is all smooth and easy.

That night, the dichotomy became surreal: there I was, in a room coated like the lunar surface with this white dust, while on the other side of the kitchen doors I could hear the jolliness of the guests.

Adding to the drama was the fact that the waitress decided not to tell any of the customers what had happened. Consequently, each time she'd return to the kitchen to pick up plates or check on a table's order, I'd note that her eyes were darting about ever more desperately, trying to imagine what to tell the customers to explain the delay.

God knows what these poor devils must have thought was going on, and with hindsight it occurs to me that the truth was probably far more benign than whatever fictions she was dispensing, but we in the restaurant trade like to feel that we have control over our worlds, and if the only control is over the truth, then we'll take that, I suppose.

Incredibly, we got through that night. We served every single guest exactly what they had ordered, though not in the time-frame they expected, and the most fascinating thing was that not one of them complained about the wait, which I don't really understand, but am grateful for to this day.

The story shows just how fast you can work when you really have to, if you keep your wits about you and stay focused, taking it one step at a time. It also offers an opportunity to evaluate the decisions that were made at each of the various crisis points. The decision to chuck the sauces, for example, was a good one, because you don't want to take the risk that they might be dangerously tainted, or even that they might not taste good. The decision to wash *everything* is one that some chefs might take exception to. With such a small staff, many of my colleagues might have decided, perhaps wisely, to wash only what they needed at the moment, and then hope for the best.

But why quibble? The good news is that everybody had dinner at Merchant House that night, nobody died, and I got a good review. And, at the end of the drama, I had a whole cellar full of wine that I could open up and with which I could obliterate the evening.

What do you eat for breakfast?
It depends on the previous evening. Too much liquid refreshment will call for bacon whereas a virtuous night will signify brioche French toast with blueberry jam.

What dish would you cook in order to seduce someone?
At my age and with my looks I think that hashish cakes would be the best bet. Alternatively, as little food as possible and a bottle of fizz.

What do you never cook?
I never cook things that I wouldn't like to eat.

What's the one dish you find hard to get right?
Most complex pastry work causes me trouble. Better delegated if at all possible.

The Next Best Thing
VINEET BHATIA

Vineet Bhatia was born in Bombay in 1967. After gaining degrees in catering and economics, he went to work for the Oberoi hotel group as an executive trainee, staying on for five years, during which time he became head chef of several restaurants within the group. When he began work in London in 1993, he was disappointed by the Indian restaurant food. In 1999, with the support of a group of investors, he opened his own restaurant, Zaika, first in Chelsea, then in Kensington High Street. In 2001, Zaika was awarded a Michelin star, making Bhatia the first Indian chef-restaurateur to receive this honour since the inception of the Guide. *In 2002, he became chef of the exotic Safran restaurant in Le Touessrok Hotel on the island of Mauritius. In 2004, he resigned from the directorship of Zaika to realise his dream: opening the restaurant Rasoi (Kitchen), along with his partner Rashima.*

WHEN I WAS a young child, I didn't have an alarm clock. I didn't need one. I was woken at six-thirty each morning by the roaring engines of the DC-10 that took off from the airport near our house in Bombay.

I still remember those aeroplanes, not only because I heard them at the beginning of each day, but also because my life's ambition then was to fly jets. I was fascinated by them. I rode to school on a bicycle and I'd pass a small flying club and stare endlessly at the Cessnas taking off and landing, marvelling at their speed and their aura of luxury.

A few years later, when I was seventeen, I took the national defence exam in the hope of joining the Air Force, but I failed the physical part of the test. They ruled me out on the grounds that I was too short in height and leg length.

They *did* offer me the opportunity to become a cadet in the Army or Navy, but my fascination for flying machines was so complete that if I couldn't be a pilot I resolved that I would do something else altogether – I applied to, and was accepted, into a catering college, and also, for good measure, obtained a degree in economics.

In hindsight, it's really quite surprising that I ended up as a chef, not only because my childhood dreams involved being a pilot, but also because I never felt that I had a natural aptitude for cooking. I tried to cook once in a while, usually in the summer holidays, because I was sensitive to the sun, so stayed indoors most of the time with my mother. She was an excellent cook with a fantastic imagination: I've never tasted food quite like hers. But despite her genes, and her early efforts to school me, I never felt that I had a knack for it.

In fact, my first few attempts at cooking on my own were downright failures.

The first was in 1977. I was ten years old and home all day on summer break. My mother and father had gone out, leaving me and my brother alone.

We were just playing around when suddenly a light bulb went off over my brother's head, and he said, with some excitement, 'Let's cook something, as a surprise for them when they come back.' He mulled this over for a moment, then snapped his fingers and said, 'Let's make them halwa!' (In case you don't know, halwa is a beloved, traditional Indian pudding.)

I thought that was a fine idea, although we soon realised that neither of us really knew how to make the pudding. We knew that it involved semolina, milk and flour, but we didn't know the proper quantities, or even the right ratio of the various ingredients to one another, so we did what any young boys would do: we decided to guess.

We melted some butter in a pot, added the semolina, and gently roasted it. Then we poured in some milk – probably three times the proper amount – and let it brew so that the milk would take on some of that caramelised flavour and taste something like fudge, or so we thought.

Before too long, it was clear that there was much too much milk and that the semolina would never absorb it, so we chucked it in the bin.

The problem was that, when you roast semolina in butter, it gives off a very nutty aroma. So when Mum came back after an hour and a half, she sniffed the air around her and said, 'Something was cooked in here. What was it?'

'Nothing, nothing, nothing,' I insisted.

But she maintained that something had been cooked. Rather than confess, I tried to convince her that perhaps she could smell something that had been cooked in our neighbour's kitchen, which in a Bombay-style apartment building is unbelievably close.

Not one to give up, my mother followed her instincts and her nose, and found her way to our discarded experiment. I would have been cleverer to have put the failed pudding down the drain and open some windows to air the place out, but I didn't, so got caught.

Another time, later that same year, I made another mistake, but this time I was more crafty. One day, when nobody was at home, I decided to bake some biscuits. I opened one of my mother's recipe books and found a recipe that called for butter and flour and sugar and stuff. I made the mixture, shaped it into very good-looking biscuits, and put them on a baking tin ready to go in the oven.

I was so excited at my imminent success that I didn't pay proper attention to the recipe's cooking temperature. I turned the heat up to 500 degrees . . . and burnt the whole lot. But I really wanted to make my family a treat, and I knew from personal experience that my mother's powerful sense of smell would find me out, so I went to a local bakery and bought a kilo of cardamom biscuits. When I got home, I put them in the oven at a low temperature to warm them, and so their aroma would overtake that of their burnt predecessors.

It worked. My mother came home, tasted the warm biscuits, and proclaimed with delight and pride that I had a talent in the kitchen.

Even after deciding on a career in the kitchen, I still had my awkward moments in restaurants, occasionally in the dining room.

In the summer of 1994, soon after I first came to London, I

was working in a restaurant and taking a management course at Westminster College every Tuesday afternoon. Those Tuesday evenings, I'd often drop into the restaurant where I worked, for a quick bite.

One night, my boss spotted me and waved me over.

'Why don't you join us?' he asked.

I took him up on his offer. He was sitting in the dining room with a couple. I don't remember the woman very well, but the man was a freckle-faced guy, unshaven, with messy hair and dirty clothes.

Who'd come to a restaurant dressed like that? I thought.

I said to him, 'What do you do for a living?'

'I play the guitar,' he answered.

I stayed there for an hour and a half, then decided I was too tired to stay any longer.

'Good luck with your guitar-playing,' I said, shaking the scruffy man's hand.

'Good luck with your cooking,' he said to me.

The next day at work, my boss came running over to me. 'You have no idea who that guy was last night, do you?'

'You're absolutely right,' I said. 'I have no idea.'

'That was Bryan Adams.'

Well, Mr Adams obviously had some luck with his guitar. And I had some luck with my cooking. There was even a time when my food was served on the Concorde, and it's served on British Airways today. It's not the same, I'm sure, as being a pilot, but in my own way I've made it to the skies nonetheless.

What do you eat for breakfast?
Wholewheat bran flakes, soya milk, fresh fruit and Verveine infusion. Need a healthy and energetic start for a hectic day. (Sometimes I cheat and nibble on my kids' chocolate-coated cereal while driving them to school.)

What dish would you cook in order to seduce someone?
My L-O-V-E dish (Left- Over Vegetables – Etc!!!).

What do you never cook?
Being a chef it's very difficult not to cook anything but what I don't like is cooking offal. I find it very awful.

What's the one dish you find hard to get right?
I used to be very uncomfortable with eggs. Fortunately I had a very military-style training and we had a fantastic executive chef who taught me the art. He said it was like making love to a women: handle them with lots of love and care. Since then I have mastered the art of making love . . . oops, sorry, eggs!

An Italian in Paris
GIORGIO LOCATELLI

Giorgio Locatelli, from Lombardy, is considered to be one of the best Italian chefs in Britain. Giorgio has been involved with several groundbreaking Italian restaurants in London, most notably Zafferano, where he earned his first Michelin star in 1999. In 2002, Giorgio and his wife, Plaxy, opened their first independent restaurant, Locanda Locatelli, which gained a Michelin star in its first year. Giorgio has a very successful TV career and has co-written a cookbook with restaurateur Tony Allan, called Tony and Giorgio. *His second book is published in 2006.*

IN 1989, after four years working at the Savoy in London, I thought it was about time I finally went to Paris. In those days Paris was like a finishing school for chefs. The only reason I'd gone to London instead was because I thought it was a lot hipper than Paris, and also because the Savoy was the place where Escoffier had cooked and developed haute cuisine.

Nowadays everyone is cooking Italian, but the big buzzword for a chef coming from Italy at that time was 'international'; we had to cook all sorts of food, especially French, and the biggest stage of all was in Paris.

So, after four years, I told the Savoy's head chef, Anton Edelmann, that I was leaving. He was pissed off at first, and didn't want me to leave. But he shared the same passion for food that I had, and he had travelled a lot by the time he was thirty, so he eventually wished me the best, even offering to set me up with a job in Paris. When he was younger, he had worked with the directors of Laurent, a famous old restaurant, and he sent me there. The pay wasn't going to be as good – in London I was a senior sous-chef, earning £400 a week, while at Laurent I was going to be a *commis rotissier* making about a third of that (and half of that would go to rent) – but I took it gladly, since it was important to me that I go to Paris.

I arrived on a Friday, with just my knives and a few chef's jackets. I had a contact there, a girl with a room for rent in the Bastille district, very central and on a direct Métro line to the restaurant. We went out for dinner, and then the next day, while wandering the city on my own, I timed the route from home to work. Twice.

On Monday morning, I was supposed to be at the restaurant at eight; I arrived at ten to seven. I sat in a café on the corner of the Champs-Elysées, ordered a *café au lait*, and looked around me, for the first time realising where I was. I have to admit I felt quite proud that I'd actually made it to Paris.

The first thing they said when I turned up at Laurent was, 'The laundry's over there.' We got four jackets and two pairs of trousers a week, so I didn't need the few things I'd brought from London. The restaurant even had a shower.

So I started work. The job of the *commis rotissier*, among other things, is to stay all afternoon when everyone else has gone off for a break, and to cook Laurent's famous *pommes soufflées*, served with châteaubriand and béarnaise sauce, a dish which has never gone off the menu.

The trick to *pommes soufflées* is to slice the potatoes exactly the right thickness, then dry them properly, so that when they hit the oil in a big pan, at just the right temperature, they puff up perfectly. You can't let them hit the bottom of the pan, or else they are ruined. Trust me – I made so many of them in the first month that the skin on my arms was bright red.

One afternoon, however, they refused to cook properly. I was supposed to have gone on my break hours before, and these fucking potatoes just would not puff up. I was getting more and more frustrated with them, when the sous-chef walked in and said, 'Well, what do you expect? You're a spaghetti. And, even worse, you learnt to cook with *les rosbifs*!'

Charming.

The irony, though, was that the same guys who called me 'spaghetti' would come and ask me questions about the classic Escoffier repertoire. At that time, a lot of French chefs had come from bourgeois restaurants outside Paris and didn't really know how to do the fancy sauces, or which garnishes went with which dishes, whereas the Savoy taught us all of them.

I learnt a lot at Laurent, though. The Savoy was a restaurant on a truly grand scale, but Laurent was a much more human size, and it showed me that it was possible, with technique and timing, to do things I would have thought were impossible for a smaller place. The cost control was amazing: the cheese cellar was run like a military operation, with twenty-five different cheeses from twenty-five different farms, and the wine list was superb. Laurent was a model of a restaurant that I could imagine running; it was a fantastic, inspiring business.

Laurent's owner was Sir James Goldsmith. When one of his daughters was getting married, naturally the reception was held in the restaurant. We had a huge, elegant multitiered wedding cake delivered. It looked like a traditional British wedding cake, but it was actually much more fragile, with layers of cream, fruit, meringue and liqueur-soaked sponge. Of course somebody managed to drop it when we took it out of the van.

This was a disaster. You can't have the boss's daughter getting married with a bashed-up cake, so we sent for an emergency *pâtissier*, who turned up with his spatula in hand, looking a bit like Donatello. I don't know whether he repaired the cake with anything edible – in fact I know there was a chunk of polystyrene in it by the time he'd finished – but it looked pretty good. In any case, we hid the broken side against an enormous vase of flowers, so we just about got away with it, although I wouldn't have liked to get the slice with the polystyrene.

Though I was eventually promoted to *chef de partie* in the fish section, money was still tight. Sometimes I got to supplement my wages with a bit of outside work, like cooking at Vincennes race course, for the Prix d'Amérique. Cash in hand was a real bonus, and it meant I could afford to go back home to Italy a couple of times a year. After one such trip, I drove my little Fiat Panda all the way back from Italy to Paris, and it was fantastic having a car in Paris. One weekend, I drove to Alain Chappel's restaurant; because he was a consultant chef for Laurent, I got to meet him. He was amazing. I even got to go to the market with him: he would visit every stall and pick up just one bunch of carrots, say, from each of them.

Anyway, I'd had a pretty good year and a half living and working in Paris – although it felt a bit provincial after London, where it was already quite rock-and-roll to be a chef; in Paris I was just a fucking cook – when I decided that I'd broaden my experience and take a job at Tour d'Argent. Also, I was eager to get a big fuck-off name on my CV.

They offered me a job as a *chef de partie* in the *garde manger*, which caused instant resentment among the French *commis* chefs, who refused to understand how a spaghetti could be a *chef de partie*. I don't think I got called by my real name once in the whole time I worked in Paris. 'Rital' was the favourite insult, but I was also called 'wop', 'spic', 'spaghetti', 'macaroni', 'chink' . . . anything but my name.

The only time I even *saw* my real name was back at Laurent, at Christmas, when we had a vote to see who would do the much-disliked job of playing Father Christmas for the kids' party in the restaurant. I checked the rubbish afterwards, and every piece of paper had my name on it. It was a conspiracy, organised by the sous-chef, who has since become a friend but back then was a bit of a bastard. The only problem, apart from the early start – Father Christmas had to come in early on Saturday – was that I didn't speak much French, so the kids probably got the wrong presents.

At Tour d'Argent, the work was much harder and more pressurised than it had been at Laurent. There were twenty-five of us in the kitchen, and another four or five in the pastry section downstairs. I thought I had made some progress while in Paris, but now I realised that, to the chefs at Tour d'Argent, I was just as much of an outsider as ever.

The head chef – I didn't like him at all – used to ask me questions about Italian cooking. At Laurent now and again I cooked Italian food – we had a dish of risotto with scallops and champagne sauce, served with Dover sole, and we used to do a bit of tagliolini, and lasagne for staff dinner – so I said I'd cook him some polenta, which I bought from a little Italian shop in the Jewish Quarter.

I brought it back to the restaurant and showed Chef and the sous-chef all the different ways you can prepare polenta – soft, hard, in diamonds, grilled – but they were unbelievable bastards. They just didn't believe Italians could cook. No matter what I did to the polenta, Chef just crossed his arms and, with a sniff, shook his head. But I refused to give up, and in the following days insisted on making it again, varying the method. The only direction I got from Chef was that he wanted it lighter. So I reduced the amount of grain that I used. 'Lighter,' he insisted. Then I made it with milk, not water. 'Lighter.' Then half cream and half milk, with lots of butter whisked in at the end . . . until eventually, one day, he said, 'Ça, c'est un vrai purée de maïs!' But it never, ever went on the menu.

One night, I was told to cook dinner for Claude Terrail, the big boss. I cooked him some brill in olive oil and grilled slices of aubergine with roast tomatoes and marjoram. When he'd finished his meal, he came into the kitchen – the first time I'd ever seen him in there – and demanded, 'Who cooked my dinner?'

I was squirming. I thought he was going to explode.

To my surprise, however, he shouted at all the other chefs,

saying that they were feeding him cream and butter every night, that they were trying to kill him, and that from now on I would be cooking his dinner every night. I was rather pleased with myself, but I didn't know then that it would lead indirectly to the greatest humiliation of my life. If Terrail hadn't liked his dinner, Chef wouldn't have done the terrine, and I wouldn't have been in the fridge . . . but I'm jumping ahead of myself.

After the episode with Terrail and his dinner, Chef said that we should do something with these vegetables that the boss had liked so much, so we added to the menu a terrine of thin slices of aubergine, courgette and peppers, layered with langoustines and set in a little jelly. A serving consisted of two slices of terrine, with three langoustines in each slice. We kept the terrines in the walk-in pastry fridge downstairs, to keep them really cold and make them easier to slice.

One day, I ran downstairs to get the next terrine, went into the fridge, and saw a chef who seemed to be bending down to look at something on the bottom shelf. I guessed it was one of the junior chefs, and I was just about to kick his arse when he stood up and turned round.

It was Chef, his moustache twitching. He had picked up a couple of button onions that he had found on the floor of the fridge, and he handed them to me. '*Tiens, tiens, petit Italien! Regards ça, rital!*' So I put the onions in my trouser pocket, without thinking, and I rushed upstairs with the terrine. He was obviously trying to make a point about wastage in the kitchen, but I wasn't really in the mood.

I carried on with the service – we were packed that night, and it went on so late that we were still sending out starters at 11.45 p.m. – and at some point I put my hand in my pocket and felt something wet and horrible. It was the two onions. I whispered, 'Old bastard!' to myself, and threw them in my bin, thinking he would have forgotten about them.

At one o'clock in the morning we had finally finished for the night. We were all changing, somebody was having a shower, when the *plongeur* came down and told us that our presence was required upstairs. I could feel that something was wrong.

We all raced up the stairs, and when we got into the kitchen, everybody was given a plastic rubbish bag to cut open and spread out on the floor at his station. By this time I realised what was happening.

I don't know whether Chef had set me up deliberately or not – maybe he thought I was getting a bit too big for my boots – but I knew that I was wrong: it might not seem like a big deal, just a couple of onions, but as a chef, if you are really dedicated, you can't throw food away. It's the same philosophy that my mother and grandmother had, and the same idea that I try to instil in the chefs who work with me now. It had crossed my mind to throw them in somebody else's bin, but I didn't, and anyway, Chef knew who he'd given the onions to.

Anyway, at this point, I was just hoping that the onions had miraculously got trapped in an empty can or something.

No such luck. As I turned my bin over on to the plastic sheet, the two onions rolled out on to the floor, and I felt like a very naughty schoolboy. Chef, who was a huge motherfucker, suddenly seemed even huger than normal. He made me feel about two feet tall. He had a big stick in his hand, like a schoolmaster or a sergeant major, so he could search through the stuff you had thrown away, and he stabbed angrily at the two onions.

I didn't say a word. I just stood there while he shouted at me.

It seemed like he shouted for hours, getting ever louder and redder in the face.

It was the biggest humiliation I have ever felt. Chef clearly got a big kick out of screaming at people: I'm sure that was his motivation, nothing to do with wastage or a philosophy of cooking, but still, I knew that I shouldn't have done it. After this, they told me every fucking day that I wasn't good enough to be a chef, and at that point I almost believed them.

I think it was at exactly that moment that I realised I didn't belong in that world. I left Tour d'Argent a couple of weeks later; I didn't even ask for a certificate. Since that day I have never again applied for a job. I didn't need the fuck-off name on my CV, either. Which, given all the shit I went through in Paris, is a little bit ironic.

I have never, since then, cooked a mousse. I have never cooked *quenelles de brochet* again, or lobster Don Carlo, which was a particularly crap dish of lobster with *sauce gribiche*.

I occasionally hire a French chef at Locanda Locatelli, mainly for the pleasure of firing him, but I have never cooked another *pomme soufflé*, and I never wear a tall hat. And I still feel just a little bit sick every time I see a button onion.

What do you eat for breakfast?
My wife and I have one apple, one banana, fresh blueberries, muesli and yoghurt; and a cup of hot water and lemon. After a couple of hours, I have my first espresso of the day.

What dish would you cook in order to seduce someone?
I don't need to cook to seduce – I have seduced already, so nowadays, I only cook for money!

What do you never cook?
Lobster – I am allergic to lobster.

What's the one dish you find hard to get right?
Some people are going to hate me for saying this, but nothing, really. I may get something wrong sometimes, but there is no difficulty in cooking.

Genus Loci

FERGUS HENDERSON

Fergus Henderson trained as an architect before becoming a chef, opening the French House Dining Room in 1992 and St John in 1995, which has won numerous awards and accolades, including Best British and Best Overall London Restaurant at the 2001 Moët et Chandon Restaurant Awards. He is the author of The Whole Beast: Nose to Tail Eating, *winner of the 2000 André Simon Award.*

IT WAS THE middle of an evening service, orders were rattling out of the printer on the pass; there was a good flow afoot. The chefs were, each and every one, full steam ahead. Suddenly a *commis* chef of a very bouncy nature gave out a cry and became more than usually agitated. Clasping her ample chest, she shouted, 'I've lost my crystal! Where's my crystal?' A matter not of the greatest urgency during the middle of a busy service, but after sending half a pot-roast pig's head for two – a thing of joy – I went to enquire what the problem was.

The *commis* chef explained: in her previous life she had worked with a vet in a large stable, during which time she had discovered a lump in one of her breasts. A real do-it-yourself kind of girl, she had dosed herself up on horse tranquilliser and proceeded to cut out the lump, and then sew the wound back up. To complete this surgery, she had nestled a healing crystal into the resultant indent. This, not surprisingly, took the kitchen somewhat aback. All chefs and kitchen porters stopped what they were doing to start looking for this far-from-ordinary stone.

Well, now that we are on our hands and knees scouring the kitchen floor for the crystal, it seems a good moment to ponder the peculiar nature of restaurants, this recent discovery putting one into a thoughtful frame of mind.

The kitchen – which in my experience is staffed by an extraordinarily diverse group of people who become an incredibly close team when dressed in their whites, inhabit a fairly inhospitable space, and produce delicious food on time at different times – is the heart of a restaurant. Even speaking as a chef, a restaurant is not just the food (though let's not forget how vital that is), but it is more. It is the 'whole catastrophe' which comes together to create the magic that can exist in a great restaurant. *Genus loci* (the spirit of time and place) is strong in the world of restaurants.

When asked to cook a grand lunch at another establishment, could we make it very St John? We were delighted. Encapsulating spring and St John perfectly, we prepared a lunch of gull's eggs and celery salt, then a slice of jellied tripe. (I know the word *tripe* strikes fear into the stomachs of many, but we have won over the most fervent antitripists with jellied tripe.) This was followed by braised squirrel and wild garlic. Gamekeepers at this time of year are culling squirrel, as they are seen as vermin, so there is much squirrel around. It is delicious and cooks very well, rather like wild rabbit.

This recipe, rather poetically with the aid of some dried ceps and the wilted garlic greens, re-created the bosky woods the squirrels came from. I popped my head out of the kitchen to see how the lunch went down, only to be met by the rather crushing comment: 'That was a very brave menu.' Now, if this lunch had taken place at St John, this comment would never have been made. It must be something to do with the musk and vibrations – the spirit of time and place.

The magic is rife, the dining room full of happy eaters, you're serving food you and your chefs love and enjoy, and that pleasure gets passed through the food to the eater. Everyone is tucking in. It's fantastic . . . Then lo and behold, we get a message that someone on table 27 says their grouse livers on toast are not grouse livers. Crash goes the magic. What's the point of cooking the rest of that person's lunch when they've just said the kitchen is lying? Where's the joy in that? I'm sure people like that get indigestion. But let us not dwell on this sour occasion.

The customer's tolerance, on the whole, is extraordinary. For example, one night pepper fell on to a hot flat-top stove, causing an evil stinging smoke, which the dumbwaiter sucked up and proceeded to exhale into the dining room. It travelled like mustard gas through the trenches, table after table being affected, triggering coughing and spluttering. Strangely, once fresh air was made available and the gas attack was over, everyone was remarkably jovial about the whole affair; this was all part of the theatre of the restaurant.

But woe betide the chef who is late with their supper! Here is where the tolerance ends. It is the interesting thing in the whole equation: timing. However much people love the food, and whatever strange smells and punishing gases they agree to wilfully endure, they want the food *on time*. This is no dinner party at home where you can placate your guest with another round of Martinis until you've put the final touches on your creation.

A waiter came into the kitchen one evening and promptly collapsed on the floor in a writhing mess, his eyes rolling back into his head. An ambulance was called, but it was evident that he needed wiser and more prudent attention than fellow waiters or chefs could administer in the short term. So we stepped out of the kitchen and yelled, 'Is THERE A DOCTOR IN THE HOUSE?' Fortunately there was one who could do right by the waiter until he was wheeled away strapped to a stretcher. Now the yelling and the stretcher seem to come under the theatre of a restaurant, not deflecting anyone's appetite, but the fact that we had *Emergency Ward 10* going on in our kitchen did not seem to alter the fact that they still wanted their mains on time.

Enough ruminating. It's time to get off my hands and knees; I can hear someone's found the crystal among a pile of oyster shells. With the crystal washed, dried, and safely returned to its cosy nook, service could resume, much to everyone's relief. Except for the floor staff. A waiter cannot say, 'I'm afraid your dinner's been held up for ten minutes because the kitchen have all had to stop to look for a healing crystal that fell out of a hole in one of the chef's breasts, due to her self-mutilation in a horsy haze.' Even though it was the truth.

Just as a last reassuring note, I met the chef some years later. She's looking very well, I'm glad to report.

What do you eat for breakfast?
Breakfast is more espresso and a cigarette than eating.

What dish would you cook in order to seduce someone?
I cooked Margot pasta, cabbage and truffle oil and we've been married for twelve years.

What do you never cook?
I don't like raw celery. I don't mind it cooked. That's as far as my cooking bias goes.

What's the one dish you find hard to get right?
Any dish when the force is not with you.

Euphoria

TAMASIN DAY-LEWIS

Tamasin Day-Lewis's cookbooks have covered a range of comforting rural recipes, from the preparation of seasonal dishes and picnics to the art of pie-baking and 'proper' slow cooking. She is the author of West of Ireland Summers *and* Last Letters Home *and is a regular contributor to* American Vogue, Vanity Fair, *and* Country Homes & Interiors. *She has directed many television documentaries.*

THE COLLEGE BUTLER had been detailed to find fine wines and sherry and to repair to my 'set' to serve them. Cambridge University has a language of its own, and when I became an undergraduate there at King's College, I learnt pretty quickly that you didn't have bedrooms or studies in your third year, you had sets comprising a sitting room complete with fireplace for toasting crumpets and teacakes from the high street's most-prized patisserie, Fitzbillies, and a bedroom – the two kept self-contained behind a stout pair of double doors.

The outside door was traditionally left ajar if you were open to callers, but closed if you were up to no good or trying to write an essay, in which case you were said to be 'sporting your oak'. There were eight similar sets on U Staircase, looking out over the River Cam, where, as all picture postcards show, students spend their summers punting, picnicking, and eschewing their studies.

We had a tiny 'gyp' room where we could cook, though its resemblance to a kitchen was not immediately apparent. I had fought hard to secure my room, U4, when booking the staircase with my posse of foodie friends; after all, if people were to ask, 'Where's Tamasin?' the reply could only be, 'In Euphoria!' As luck would have it, my rooms were also closest to the kitchen.

So, the butler had appeared with white-starched linen table-cloth and napkins that would have stood as frostily to attention as anything at Le Cirque or one of the great temples to cuisine; the bottles were on their way, presently being chambréd in the bowels of the college kitchen; all I had to do was prepare a dinner the likes of which no student had prepared in the collective living memories of the dons about to attend it. A Roman feast. Would I have attempted this Everest of a task if I had known that disaster was about to strike? That I cannot say, but I can tell you that this picture of order and organisation, of tradition and good taste, was about to be blown apart by my combination of ignorance and ambition.

What had I let myself in for? The confidence of youth, the not knowing what you don't know, the desire to show off and not be like the other students eating pigswill in hall every night or stirring packet soup into chipped mugs in their rooms; spooning cold rice pudding from the tin, surviving on toasted sandwiches from a tiny café opposite the austerely beautiful world-famous façade of Cambridge's best-known college, founded by Henry VI, who also founded Eton.

Having been accepted as one of the first women at King's when they decided to go coeducational after centuries as an all-male domain, here I was trying to introduce a more female take on its world of entertaining, away from the world of the 'top table' that the dons dined ceremoniously at every night in their gowns, sweeping in like great flapping birds for Latin grace, to plunder the college's world-class wine cellar, and partake of its grim, institutional apology for good food.

Here I was, about to preside over a lavish dinner party despite the exigencies of my student grant, with a burgeoning sense that the women in the college should be responsible for transforming this previously all-male bastion into a more homely, civilised place where fine dining and good wines could coexist, and even become de rigueur.

The rampant, politically correct feminist student lobby would have been horrified had they known of my belief in the civilising effects of a good dinner or the fact that I was prepared to cook for as many boys and girls on my staircase as wanted to dine every night. The feminists were busy trying to get a condom machine installed in the girl's cloakroom on the grounds that it was sexist if there was one only in the boy's. Meanwhile I was learning about budgeting; how to buy cheap cuts of scrag of lamb or choose between the end-of-the-day's fruit and vegetables in the market at a discount, and making sure there was some sort of equal distribution of labour when I cooked; that the boys brought the wine, washed up, even went shopping from time to time.

Hell, I didn't want to pander to the well-known soubriquet of being a 'bluestocking', the barely veiled insult that still exists to describe the confirmed spinster in academics whose eccentricity, unworldliness, and unforgivingly plain looks only the rarefied and obscure sanctuary of an Oxford or Cambridge college could absorb.

At this point, I should probably explain my suitability for the task ahead. When I left home for university, I could cook an omelette. And that is just about it. It was, however, a very good omelette; my mother had taught me that it took precisely fifty-five seconds to cook THE PERFECT OMELETTE, exactly how long it took to recite a Shakespeare sonnet. Not so odd a comparison given that my father, C. Day Lewis, was the poet laureate; I have no doubt that my mother probably recited the bard's canon of sonnets by memory as she worried the buttery eggs in the pan with her palette knife and flipped them out with the desired *centres baveux* and perfectly pale primrose undersides.

My limited repertoire at this stage was understandable. My mother dominated her tiny kitchen and it was not a place where there could ever be room for two cooks. My experiments were confined to pressing the extra bits of pastry remaining from one of her tarts firmly into small patty tins until they were so overworked and greasy and thick that they came out of the oven half raw, the burnt, bubbling jam – no child ever learns less is more – erupting Vesuvially and stickily and breaching the pastry walls and then eaten so hot by me and my brother that it welded itself to the roofs of our mouths, or else scraping the last bits of cake mixture raw from the bowl when she'd made one of her weekly teatime treats and eating it straight from the wooden spoon.

Though I had been brought up in a house with a tradition of

good food, I never really wanted to learn to cook. As a child, it didn't occur to me that it might be an interesting or exciting thing to do. Eating was always the pleasure. My grandparents, unusually for the time, kept a marvellous, traditional English table, and their cook, the redoubtable Rhoda Fisher, was still busy turning out three meals if not four a day well into her seventies. My grandmother did what ladies in her position did, which was to know all about good food, to order exactly what she wanted when the cook went into my grandfather's dressing room every morning to discuss the day's menu, even to know the ingredients of every dish she ordered, but to have never actually cooked anything herself.

There was an apocryphal story about her first dinner party when she married my grandfather. She was all of seventeen and had no idea how to address the cook or what to order, but felt she'd better not let on. There were going to be ten people at the party that evening. Quick as a flash, when asked what should be bought for dinner, my grandmother replied, 'Ten pounds of fillet steak.'

By the time I was born, she'd had nearly three decades of practice and as long to cultivate the other imperative qualification, greed, a must-have for any serious cook or bon vivant and one which hasn't bypassed anyone in at least four generations of my family, including my own three children.

And so it was that one dinnertime when I had been allowed to stay up, although it was not given to me actually to dine with my grandparents, my grandfather ate his bloodily rare grouse served *à l'ancienne* with fresh peppery watercress, game chips, bread sauce, fried breadcrumbs and gravy and then asked me if I'd like to try it. I was given the carcass and remember only the thrill, the indefinable thrill of a new taste so transporting and beyond the realms of any expectation that for a minute you wonder that something can defy even your imagination. I picked every tiddly bone clean as though it were the last supper and have continued to do so with game birds and bones of any sort throughout my life. That night was like a shaft of light into a secret world, a grown-up world of taste whose discovery was going to alter the way I thought about food from thereon in. Somewhere the thought lodged in my brain that good food was all about good ingredients and good cooking. Perhaps I ought to find out how to cook.

I began the next term at school not even realising that recipes were there for a purpose, that weighing and measuring were a means to a delicious end, that only the best and most experienced of cooks could cook without paying attention to such trifling little details. I purchased a bottle of Ribena. I managed to get to the local tuck shop and buy cream, icing sugar, and a lemon. I stuck my head through the school kitchen window and begged Chef for an ice tray, promising to return it and cajoling him into helping me in my mission. Blackcurrant juice, cream and lemon were stirred into a putrid pink mixture as thick as paint and poured into the ice tray. I carried it gingerly back to Chef, who promised to freeze it for me. That night I collected the frozen pink ice cream and took it proudly back to my dormitory to tempt my dorm mates with. It was toothachingly sweet and sickly with cream, but the funny thing was I didn't see it as a complete disaster; it was an experiment, and that meant critical faculties had to be employed, as did that thing I was unaware existed at that stage, the palate. Next time I would use more lemon, less sugar, and less cream. I might even read a recipe book and find out how to make *real* blackcurrant ice cream.

My mother, unlike my grandmother, did not have a cook;

indeed, she had had a rude awakening on marrying my father coming from this world of cooks and housekeepers, governesses and maids. My father insisted on having a pudding every night. My mother had to rise to the challenge, and on the first night presented my father with pancakes. Child's play, you might think. No one had told her that you didn't use self-raising flour to make pancake batter, so the slim pancakes she'd aspired to flipping and folding and spritzing with lemon juice and sugar were not quite as she'd imagined them to be. My father looked at the sorry, grey leather effigies on his plate and hurled one against the wall, where it stuck, proclaiming that it looked exactly like Keats's death mask.

Perhaps these stories from two generations of women in my family were the things that spurred me on, made me realise that failure, kitchen disaster, was not only an option, it was a given. It didn't mean you should give up, that you were a bad cook; at worst you could dine out on the stories and tell them to your children and grandchildren; at best you would improve as a result.

My only real memory of cooking for my father, who died when I was eighteen, was an occasion more disastrous than my mother's first. It was something of a warm-up act and wake-up call for me to finally get down to learning the basics, understanding the importance of technique and how to read a recipe.

My mother had gone away and asked me to cook for my father and I, presuming that there was really no great skill or knowledge required, and oblivious to timing and technique, pronounced I would fry some aubergines to go with the lamb chops that I assumed just needed a little cremating under the grill.

I cut the spongy purple grenades into fat wedges and plunged them into a pan of oil, oil not even hot enough to begin the frying process. It wasn't long before the oily bath seemed to have disappeared and things began to smoke. I poured a further libation of oil into the hot pan. This time the aubergines seemed to be turning dusky brown rather too quickly. I thought I'd better drain them and remove them before it was too late. My father cut into the resistant brown discs. They managed to be as tough and hard as to almost appear raw at the same time as to be leaking oil like a tanker that had struck rock. They were so oily that even with copious amounts of kitchen paper they were inedible; but my father never breathed a word and, like a fellow conspirator, never even let on to me that my burnt offering was unacceptable.

Other than the school cookery lessons that were supposed to teach us the rudiments of good baking and where I excelled only in the greed department, I had had little experience of proper cooking when I left the fold for the portals of King's. In between *Sir Gawain and the Green Knight*, Greek tragedy, the metaphysical poets, Milton, and Chaucer, I read Elizabeth David and Jane Grigson, the two seminal food writers of the time: Mrs David for her prose and her discovery of the great regional, provincial cooking of France and Italy and the Mediterranean, and Mrs Grigson, the scholar cook, for her more detailed instruction and the inspiration of recipes that always worked whatever your level of knowledge. And I had a boyfriend at King's who was as interested in good food as I was. He showed serious skill and a rather more sophisticated knowledge of food that didn't just amount to having good taste.

The reason for holding my first proper dinner party was simple. The avuncular and kindly figure of the senior librarian at King's, Tim Munby, invited me and a couple of friends to dinner, which his wife, Sheila, had cooked, and we had been entertained as though we were serious grown-ups, not just starved, troublesome students. During the course of dinner, Tim mentioned that, in all his years at King's of giving similar dinners to a few select freshmen, not one student had ever returned the invitation. Here was a challenge I could take up.

I decided to meet it with a couple of the friends who had also been so generously entertained. I sent out invitations and decided that if we put the booze on the college bill, at least I wouldn't have to pay for it until the following term. The next thing was the menu. We could hardly serve the sausage and mash, belly of pork and beans, pig's liver with root vegetables, or Irish stew that were our U Staircase staples. A stroke of luck happened the weekend before the dinner.

An old friend who was a good shot had descended on King's with a brace of pheasants for me to roast. This was not only free food, it was the kind of food befitting the kind of banquet I intended to give. I was planning the traditional English accompaniments to a brace of roast pheasants: bread sauce, roast potatoes and parsnips, carrots Vichy, dark onion gravy made with the giblets and a slug of red wine. My boyfriend could make the crème caramel, one of the cheapest puddings in the book; I would buy some cheese in the market, and the King's cellar would do the rest.

My friend had arrived with the brace of birds, and, having not been brought up as au fait as he to the world of hunting, shooting, and fishing, I didn't even ask him what to do with them. I was wholly unaware of the extent of my ignorance. At least I wasn't squeamish like many of my friends about livers and gizzards and paunching and gutting. I hung the beautiful brace from the ceiling and believed that was all there was to it.

So there I was, transforming my study into a dining room with a borrowed table and the stiffest college linen. The kitchens had agreed to lend me a few serving dishes and I was going to beg, borrow, or steal the cutlery and plates from the pantry. I went downstairs to get started. I switched on the tiny Baby Belling stove that would just about contain the roasting pan with the pheasants and vegetables. Other than that, there was an electric ring on top of the stove and a gas ring on the worktop. The small fridge the eight of us shared was frequently raided at night by teams of stoned, marauding students who probably knew well that if anyone was likely to have rashers and eggs and scrumptious leftovers it would be U Staircase. The vegetables were still there. I peeled and prepared them all and put them in my battered, secondhand pans. Time to get to work on the birds.

I remember opening a large black bin bag and pulling the pheasants' feathers in clumps down into it. As I got closer to skin and flesh, it all seemed rather peculiar. The normal pink goosebumpy look of the skin wasn't quite as it should be. In fact it was a rather livid shade of green. The worst horror was yet to come. The side of one of the birds was actually moving. Moving as in covered with maggots. Alive!

It is one of those bad jokes told in English aristocratic circles that a pheasant isn't hung enough until you can scrape the maggots from the flesh. How could I not have realised that, cold as the gyp room was, the ambient temperature was not at preservation level? I remember dropping the hideous brace of birds into the bin and shrieking. The game was up. I mean, the game was off. We had nothing for dinner. What to do? The guests were arriving in a couple of hours and this was before the days of late-night or all-night shopping;

Cambridge shut down firmly at 5.30 p.m., the market even earlier.

I have no memory of where we found a chicken to roast (although I know we didn't wring its neck or pluck it ourselves). And can you feast, indeed banquet, on the everyday common or garden bird? Of course you can and of course we did. The bird's interior succulence offset by its startlingly crisped, salted, bronzed skin, the bread sauce creamy with its scent of clove and nutmeg, the sweet parsnips caramelised in the bird's juices, the potatoes as crunchy as you could wish for. The disaster was all mine. The guests need never have been made aware of it, but that would have been cheating.

The more experienced one becomes in the kitchen, the less one is inclined to show off. I would as soon invite people to eat a plain risotto or bowl of pasta as I would a roast woodcock or wild salmon *en croute*. Simple food cooked well with good ingredients cannot diminish the occasion of bringing friends to the table, good wine, good conversation, and the fact that you have gone to all that effort in the first place. Besides, I never learnt anything from the successes, except that I would still always wonder afterwards, couldn't I have crisped that skin a bit more, taken that tart out two minutes earlier, upped the spicing, used less lemon juice or cream?

Such is the nature of the passionate cook, even at the fledgling stage. And, as Samuel Beckett so succinctly put it, forbidding us to dwell on our disasters or give up, 'Try again, fail again, fail again better.'

What do you eat for breakfast?
Breakfast is hot water and Seggiano chestnut honey after a six-mile run.

What dish would you cook in order to seduce someone?
Food to seduce is entirely dependent upon mood, season, the person and their desires. I cook to seduce my boyfriend every time I cook for him, whatever the food, whatever the occasion. There is nothing less likely to seduce than obvious seduction food presented aphrodisiac-style. Sticky ribs eaten with the fingers or cake dripping with passion-fruit curd is far more seductive than asparagus spears with melted butter, which is so obvious. Food you can play with and feed and cover your lover with, well, you have to be in the right mood for that – no one wants to have melted chocolate dripping from their best frock or shirt! I hate questions like this, they are *so* unsexy.

What do you never cook?
Rice pudding and green peppers, or any food I *really* dislike.

What's the one dish you find hard to get right?
There is no one dish. I am constantly trying to improve every dish I cook.

A Simple Request
SAMUEL CLARK

Samuel Clark works with his wife, Samantha Clark. They met at the Eagle gastropub, and then worked together at the River Café. They spent their honeymoon touring Morocco and Spain, then opened Moro in the Clerkenwell district of London in 1997, with their associates Mark Sainsbury and Jake Hodges. The restaurant won both the Time Out *and* BBC Good Food *awards for Best New Restaurant. Sam and Sam Clark are authors of* The Moro Cookbook *and* Casa Moro: The Second Cookbook.

IN THE LATE 1980s, when I was a young cook just out of cooking college, not yet employed in a restaurant, the art dealer Adrian Ward-Jackson, a friend of my mother, informed me that he was having Princess Margaret round to dinner.

'Perhaps you'd like to cook for us,' he suggested very sweetly, downplaying the enormity of the suggestion.

How could I resist?

'Great. Sure,' I said, attempting to contain my excitement.

When the day of the dinner arrived, I shopped for the freshest and finest of ingredients, as befitted a royal affair such as this, and then made my way to Adrian's flat in Mayfair. It was beautiful, modest in scope but very richly and ornately decorated. Adrian also dealt in antiques, so the sitting room was crowded with paintings, sculptures, and various objets d'art. And the overall design of the home was the equal of the collection it housed; every fabric was textured; every surface perfectly polished. Despite the lavish decor, it was remarkably cosy, and had the effect of putting one quite at ease, rather than being intimidating.

The kitchen, too, was delightful, done up in wonderful découpage. For instance, the refrigerator was made to look like a bookcase lined with clothbound classics; but when you pulled at the door it of course opened and inside were the bright, fully functioning shelves of a refrigerator.

In preparation for the evening, I had made a number of careful decisions, all of them intended to eliminate any element of risk. I hadn't yet worked in restaurants or developed my own personal style, so for the menu, I turned to the dishes most cooking students would make: I prepared a soup (though I can't for the life of me remember what kind), and a rack of lamb with potatoes Dauphinoise, and a rhubarb fool for pudding.

My goal was to prepare a meal that could be described as unadventurous but delicious, if only ultimately of very average quality. Put another way: my mission was not to embarrass myself.

To remove any lofty expectations, I even downplayed my culinary education, dressing for the occasion in a beautiful shirt and apron, in no way indicative of any professional training.

My clothes and the menu were also intended to make me as

comfortable as possible. I had been cooking in a home setting since I was a child, so I created the environment to which I was accustomed.

By all accounts, as the dinner hour approached, my plan seemed to be working. I spent the better part of the afternoon making the meal at a relaxed pace, feeling quite at ease. Adrian left me alone, though I could hear him moving about, talking on the telephone, and so on.

Finally, I heard the Princess arrive and felt a tingle of excitement. A member of the royal family was going to be enjoying a meal prepared by my hand! I was confident that she would enjoy it because most of the dishes were nearly finished: the lamb was attaining a lovely burnished golden-brown exterior in the oven; the soup was done and keeping nicely warm, even the rhubarb fool had been set to cool in the traditional long-stemmed, glass wine goblets that show off its brilliant ruby-red colour.

Adrian's home was designed so that one passed the kitchen on the way in from the front door to the dining room. As Adrian and the Princess approached, I again felt a twinge of giddiness. No sooner had they passed than Adrian appeared, stuck his head in the door, and casually whispered, 'Oh, by the way, I'd like to have some biscuits with pudding,' before disappearing again, following after the Princess.

What's that? I thought. Did he just say 'biscuits'? How odd, because we'd never discussed them.

Panic set in quickly. Christ, I thought. Biscuits! What am I going to do?

I hadn't planned for them, I hadn't brought along the necessary ingredients, and – if I'm honest – didn't really know *how* to make biscuits, not being a pastry cook and not having any recipe books with me.

I can't very well march out there and tell them that I don't know how to make bloody biscuits, now, can I?

Adrian had employed a waiter for the evening and I sent the first course, the soup, out with him. As Adrian and Princess Margaret began their meal, I rooted hurriedly through the cupboards to see what ingredients I had at my disposal to pull off this last-minute request. The découpage didn't seem quite so charming as all of a sudden my carefully laid plans were turning to rubbish.

In one of the cupboards, I found a box of inexpensive gingersnaps of completely unremarkable quality.

I studied the box in my hand, thinking, OK, how can I make these taste different, better than they are?

On the counter, I spied a bottle of brandy and snapped my fingers.

I've got it!

I laid the biscuits out in a glass baking dish and drizzled enough brandy over them to submerge them. Then I set them aside to let them soak.

When the waiter returned a little while later, I sent him out with the lamb and potatoes, and concentrated on finishing the pudding. As I began to lift a biscuit from the dish, however, I discovered that it had become hopelessly limp, tearing in half like a soggy sheet of newspaper.

Hurriedly, I turned on the oven, still hot from the lamb, delicately transferred the biscuits to a baking sheet with the aid of a spatula, and slid them inside.

It was a torturous situation: I had no time to lose, and yet I had to keep the heat relatively low, for fear of burning the things – or perhaps even igniting the alcohol. That would've been a truly fine mess, starting a fire in Adrian's miniature museum.

Time was ticking away and I stood shaking my head impatiently and looking into the oven, whispering to the gingersnaps, 'Dry, you bastards. Dry.'

Finally, I couldn't delay the pudding any longer. I took the biscuits out of the oven, only to discover that they were still limp and soggy. As the waiter looked on in bemusement, I fanned them with my hand, trying to get them to dry just a little bit more, but it was hopeless.

I plated the biscuits, which were slightly hard around the edges and mushy in the centre, with an alcoholic aroma emanating from them, and sent them out along with the glasses full of rhubarb fool.

To take my mind off what must be transpiring in the dining room, I began cleaning up the kitchen, scrubbing the pots and pans and returning the ingredients, including that box of gingersnaps, to their proper homes.

A few minutes later, a figure appeared in the kitchen door, but this time it wasn't the waiter; it was Adrian himself – holding the empty biscuit plate in his hands. With a twinkle in his eye, Adrian said, 'Her Highness would love some more biscuits.' Then he disappeared back into the dining room.

It was an unbelievable turn of events. I could scarcely fathom how the appalling biscuits had been so well received. Not that it mattered much at that point. My astonishment was instantly replaced by the realisation that . . . *Christ! I have to go through all that again*!

Hastily, I dug the box of gingersnaps out of the cupboard, sprinkled the bloody things with brandy, shoved them in the oven, took them out, fanned them like an idiot, and plated them, noisily bumping around the kitchen as if I were performing in some sort of vaudeville.

To this day, I don't know if Adrian and his royal guest were having a bit of fun at my expense. Perhaps, as I've sometimes imagined, they flushed the biscuits down the toilet and were only asking for a second serving as a sort of private, though good-natured, joke.

When Adrian was seeing the Princess to the door, she stopped at the kitchen to say, 'Thank you for a lovely meal.'

I wanted to ask if she really had liked the biscuits, but there simply wasn't any appropriate way of doing so.

'You're very welcome, Your Highness,' I said. 'I'm glad you enjoyed it.'

I suppose I could have asked Adrian but I decided to leave it alone. It was awfully nice of him to give me such an opportunity and, if they were having a laugh at my expense, then it was richly deserved, the least I could do to say thank you.

What do you eat for breakfast?
Soggy cereal left by the children.

What dish would you cook in order to seduce someone?
Tagliarini with white truffles.

What do you never cook?
Spam.

What's the one dish you find hard to get right?
Soufflé.

Grace under Pressure
ANTONY WORRALL THOMPSON

Antony Worrall Thompson was born in 1951 in Stratford-upon-Avon. He owns the Notting Grill in Holland Park and the Kew Grill, Richmond, which specialise in organic meat, fish and vegetables, and is a partner in Angel Coaching Inn and Grill, at Heytesbury near Warminster, where his mission is to source the best local food. His books include The Small and Beautiful Cookbook, Supernosh *with wine writer Malcolm Gluck,* Modern Bistro Cooking, Healthy Eating for Diabetes, Real Family Food *and* GL Diet Made Simple. *He regularly guests-presents and cooks on the Food Channel's* Good Food Live, *and is the presenter of BBC1's* Saturday Kitchen. *In 2003, he gained widespread popularity through his appearances on ITV's* I'm a Celebrity Get Me Out of Here.

THERE WAS A TIME, many years ago, when I used to sit in traffic jams, pulling my hair out, becoming ever more frustrated that I was being delayed. Then one day it occurred to me: there's nothing to be done. Worrying, panicking and hair-pulling don't help things at all.

It's a lesson I learnt in traffic, but it's helped me immeasurably in the kitchen. There's simply no value in losing one's cool, and I've been reminded of this over and over again. Keeping a cool head has kept me in the game and seen me through more than a few crises.

For instance, there was the time, in the late 1970s, when I was contracted to cater for a Jewish wedding in London's Temple. This was in the days before I was able to hire drivers, so while my servers went there directly, I myself loaded the van at my catering warehouse, and drove it to the venue.

Well, there was no traffic on this particular day, but I happened to be running late, and so was driving faster than usual. Coming over Westminster Bridge, I took a sharp right and hit the central reservation: the entire buffet meal came crashing off the shelves and on to the (thankfully immaculate) floor – a variety of salads, whole cooked salmons, ribs of beef, and so on – they all found their way down.

I really speeded up at that point, because now there were miracles to be performed. As I drove down the Embankment, I could see the bride and groom leaving the chapel, clearly having just said, 'I do.' They were followed closely by their 300 or so guests, who proceeded to make their way down a receiving line, and to pose for photographs of various groups and sub-groups.

As all of this transpired, I surreptitiously went to work in the reception room. With the help of my servers, salads were recomposed, and the sides of beef were snapped into place as if by chiropractors. Two of the salmons were discovered to be intact; the other two, I converted to mousse with the aid of a bit of cream, some herbs and a mixer, but didn't present them until after the happy couple had been served from the whole salmons they had ordered during the wedding planning.

It was my good fortune that day that a number of guests were on diets, so not terribly hungry. In fact, everyone was so delighted with the meal that I was asked to give a little talk after the luncheon.

Perhaps my ability to stay cool in a crisis has served me a little *too* well, because I'm now a bit of a walking disaster, and I'm so at peace with that role that it's become an expected part of almost any appearance I make. For instance, I've set more than a few tea towels ablaze on TV. It seems I'm always leaving them on the side of my stove a bit too close to the lighted ring. If you've seen me on *Ready, Steady, Cook*, then you know this is true.

I'm also constantly blowing the lid off liquidizers when blending hot liquids. I simply was never taught that processing hot liquid in a small sealed container creates a powerful vacuum capable of shooting the cover off like a cannonball.

Then there was the time when we used to shoot my television programme, *Saturday Kitchen*, live at my house. Before coming on the air, we always turned the gas on and heated the pots and pans to save time during the actual show.

One Saturday, I had some onions sweating in oil and butter, but I clearly got too much of a head start because when we began the broadcast and lifted the lid they were all terribly scorched. Fortunately, since we were in my own kitchen at home, I was able to grab another pan and another onion and quickly start again; had we been in a studio, with its fake kitchen, I wouldn't have been able to get hold of an onion from the empty cupboards and cabinets.

Everything seemed fine, but what I didn't know was that the

smoke created by the onions triggered my silent alarm system, which made an automated call to the fire station. While we were on the air, the fire brigade came hurtling into my front yard, sirens howling and everything.

That little incident aside, I have to be honest: I sometimes blow the lid off a liquidiser or let those tea towels catch fire on purpose. I think viewers like to see a chef like me make mistakes because they think, If he can do it, then I can do it. That's the idea of this book, isn't it – that we all make mistakes in the kitchen? Which reminds me: when I do catch a tea towel on fire, my preferred method of extinguishing the flames is to scrunch the towel in my hands, smothering it with my bare flesh. When I do this, Ainsley, my host and presenter, always says the same thing, and it's especially apt: 'Now, don't try that at home, children, don't try that at home.'

What do you eat for breakfast?
Porridge or muesli. Sometimes I have a bowl of berries with yoghurt.

What dish would you cook in order to seduce someone?
Sexy toffee banana pudding.

What do you never cook?
Rice pudding!

What's the one dish you find hard to get right?
Pastry – particularly shortcrust.

Lean Times at the Fat Duck
HESTON BLUMENTHAL

One of our most celebrated culinary figures, self-taught chef Heston Blumenthal opened the Fat Duck in 1995 in Bray, Berkshire. The Michelin Guide awarded the Fat Duck its first star in 1999, and upheld it in 2000 and 2001. He was awarded a second star in 2002, and a third star in 2004. Blumenthal was the first winner of the Chef of the Year award in the 2001 Good Food Guide. His first book, Family Food, *was published in 2001, the same year he hosted the programme* Kitchen Chemistry *on the Discovery Channel.*

M Y RESTAURANT, the Fat Duck, currently possesses three Michelin stars, a fact of which I am exceedingly proud. I'm all the more gratified when I look back on our formative period, about a decade ago, and remember the many incredible struggles that faced me every day. Those were pretty damn tricky times, to say the least . . .

Thanks to the physical space itself – a copper bar originally built in 1550 as part of a cottage, which had been a pub since the 1600s – the Fat Duck was challenging from the start. It had low ceilings, just over seven feet high, with beams that made the room seem even smaller. Though we did a refurbishing, modernising the space and painting the walls for a stony effect, it was still a very old building. In fact, it was so old that the loo was outside. I'm quite sure that we were the only restaurant with an outside toilet to receive a Michelin star.

When we first opened, the dining room was a rather spartan affair. There were no tablecloths. The wine list could be printed on a single piece of paper, with only twenty whites, twenty reds, and a small selection of sparkling and dessert wines. Equally minimal was the staff – a new restaurant is faced with special challenges, since, if you have no name and no money in the bank, it's difficult to attract the best employees. So that initial year it was just me and a pot washer in the kitchen, with three front-of-house people in the dining room.

One of the most telling aspects of the early days of the Fat Duck was our system of communicating with the dining-room team. The kitchen was situated behind the dining room, separated by a small passageway furnished with only a bench, where a staff member could take a *very brief* respite on especially busy nights, perhaps while waiting for the final dish to complete a table's order.

Between the passageway and the kitchen was a pass-through window. When the food went up on the pass, I'd do a quick double-clap to get the attention of a waiter or the maître d' from the dining room. It was a rapid little sound that customers didn't notice, but to which the service team's ears had become highly attuned.

In time, our business began to get more robust, and I needed more help in the kitchen. Unable to attract any cooks of note, I found myself hiring a not-insignificant number of lowlifes: axe murderers, bank robbers, and the like. (Well, not quite – at least, no *convicted* axe murderers and bank robbers.) Anyone I could lure and satisfy with my unavoidably meagre wages was fair game, including one chap who had been in army prison for a time and was trying to straighten out his life. He was huge, six foot six, with humongous, gnarly hands and a coating of tattoos over his entire body. Though only twenty-one, he gave the impression of a soul who had lived a long and tortured existence.

My motley crew in the back were offset by the front-of-house employees – the ones that the customers actually saw. Thankfully, this contingent was infinitely more presentable. There was a French waiter who showed a lot of promise. And there was an English maître d' who had worked at a two-Michelin-star restaurant in London and was very good at his job. He was thirty-five years old, balding, impeccably dressed, and very well spoken. He did have some affectations, but I found them charming. For example, like many people who had worked in French restaurants, he had developed a habit of ending his sentences with a little 'unh' sound to imitate the cadence of French language, such as 'More bread, unh.' Or 'I'm going over here, Chef, unh.'

He was a true service master, fastidious almost to a fault, and would walk the dining-room floor, straightening curtains, always busying himself with the betterment of the establishment.

But then something happened, and it crushed him: he had a very young girlfriend who had gone off to university. A practical person, he was quite prepared for her to meet a younger man.

Instead, while she was home on holiday, she went to a party, fell in love with his best friend, also thirty-five, and ran off with him.

That he wasn't prepared for, and he lost it. I didn't realise how badly until one particular evening.

This was a Saturday and we were serving about fifty-five people, a very busy night for us. My team of criminals was working like mad. I was putting the proper finish on every dish before setting it up on the pass and doing my little double-clap, whereupon a front-of-house staff member would arrive and retrieve the plates.

At one point, round about eight o'clock, I put some plates up on the pass, and did the double-clap.

Nobody came.

I did it again. *Clap-clap*. And again. *Clap-clap*.

Finally, I pounded twice on the pass itself. *BANG-BANG!* Not very quiet at all. I'm sure some customers heard that one.

But still nobody came.

For me, and for many chefs, to leave the kitchen during service is a nightmare. Not only does it slow you down, but you lose your flow and concentration – and you don't know what crisis might be waiting for you when you return. And yet I had no choice. I stalked out of the kitchen and into the dining room to see where my staff had disappeared to.

No sooner did I arrive on the service floor than I spotted my maître d' standing over a table of three customers, laughing it up and having a good old time, completely oblivious to the operation of the restaurant.

I was positively fuming, but I had other priorities, so I made a mental note to deal with it later. Then I asked one of the waiters to come back to the kitchen and fetch the food, and got on with my evening.

When I had finished cooking for the night, I had to run through the dining room, up the stairs to the restaurant office, and phone in orders to purveyors for the next day, before they closed.

As I made the trip, I passed a table of four – two men and two women – seated by the foot of the stairs. From their slouchy posture and uproarious laughter it was clear that they'd had quite a bit of wine.

One of the men drunkenly grabbed my arm as I passed by.

'We have to tell you, we think your maître d' is great,' he slurred.

'Do tell,' I said, trying to be every bit the charming, unruffled chef, but still crossly remembering the way the maître d' had disappeared on me earlier.

'Well,' the man went on. 'He does the most amazing impression of Basil Fawlty.'

I feigned laughter, simmering under my cool countenance, and sought out more information. 'How's that?'

'Well,' the man said, the rest of his party already erupting in laughter at what was coming. 'We were sitting here when a party of four came in the door. They asked your maître d' if you had a table for four.'

The storyteller paused here because he was too overcome with laughter to continue. 'And then,' he said, still struggling to compose himself. 'And then,' he said, turning red with laughter. 'And *then*,' he said, finally getting on with it, 'your maître d' looks left, looks right, looks up, looks down, and says, "No, we haven't!"'

The four of them burst into fits of laughter, banging on the table as though it were the funniest thing they had ever heard.

'*Then*,' the man said, his shoulders shaking, 'he walked off saying, "F—ing customers. F—ing customers."'

They all started slamming the table harder and convulsing with laughter, barely able to breathe now.

I felt as if someone had just lit a bonfire in my stomach. Out of politeness, I forced a little chuckle and headed up the stairs to do my ordering.

I had hardly picked up the phone when the French waiter appeared. 'Chef, can you come downstairs?'

'When?'

'Now, please.'

I hurried down the stairs, through the dining room, and into the passageway to the kitchen. Sitting there on the bench was the maître d', with his head in his hands, rocking back and forth.

'What on earth are you doing?' I demanded, pretty fed up with his odd behaviour.

He removed his hands, revealing a big red lump on his forehead.

'He hit me,' he cried, indicating the tattooed behemoth in the kitchen.

Before I could gather more facts for myself, the French waiter pulled me aside and explained what had happened.

A call had come in, and in those days when the front-of-house phone was engaged the incoming call would automatically divert to a phone on the wall outside the kitchen. It was too far from the pass for me to reach it, but this hulking figure had no problem – he had stretched out with his big, meaty arms and answered the phone in his frightening, dungeon-master's voice: 'Good evening, Fat Duck.'

It was a customer, seeking a booking. The cook put the call on hold and, at that moment, the maître d' had come into the passageway.

'I've a booking for you,' said the cook, taking the phone off hold.

'I don't want to speak to any f—ing customers,' said the maître d'. 'They're all f—ing idiots.'

Rightly fearful that the customer on the phone could hear this, the cook stretched out his arm, trying to put his hands over the mouth of the maître d' and silence him. Instead, he succeeded in striking him smack on the forehead, sending him reeling back on to the bench.

Taking the waiter's word as gospel – and really, who else could I trust in this situation? – I exonerated the cook and blamed the maître d' for the whole ugly incident.

I had no choice. The next morning, I sacked the maître d', giving him two weeks' notice.

The funny thing is, a lot has changed at the Fat Duck since that night. We now have a loo inside the building. The wine list is a book – rather than a scrap of paper – reflecting the formidable cellar we've built up. We have beautiful leather-backed chairs and three Michelin stars. We make enough money and have enough of a reputation to snare the best possible staff.

We've made it, as they say.

But I would still hire this chap today – and I would still end up having to let him go. In the restaurant business, as in life, you can only have so much control over your fate. At some point, you're at the mercy of the universe.

And of your f—ing employees.

What do you eat for breakfast?
I start every morning with the same thing, a bowl of porridge with skimmed milk.

What dish would you cook in order to seduce someone?
I remember once before I became a chef I cooked Zanna madeleines, which she loves, and it must have worked because she married me.

What do you never cook?
I enjoy cooking everything, all types of food. However, I'd never use poor-quality ingredients.

What's the one dish you find hard to get right?
I am never truly satisfied: you can always improve on a dish. At the Fat Duck it can take up to eighteen months for a dish to make it on to the menu, but it doesn't stop there. Even once a dish has made it to the menu we are still learning and developing, so dishes are continually evolving.

Horror in Gerona
FERRÁN ADRIÀ

Ferrán Adrià began his famed culinary career, washing dishes at a French restaurant in the town of Castelldefels, Spain. He has since worked at various restaurants, served at the Spanish naval base of Cartagena, and in 1984, at the age of twenty-two, joined the kitchen staff of El Bulli. Only eighteen months later, he became head chef of the restaurant – which went on to receive its third Michelin star in 1997. Adrià's gift for combining unexpected contrasts of flavour, temperature and texture has won him global acclaim as one of the most creative and inventive culinary geniuses in the world; Gourmet magazine has hailed him as 'the Salvador Dalí of the kitchen'.

'THE LOBSTERS ARE off,' said the voice on the other end of the telephone.

This was *not* good news: *Off* is the word we in the culinary business use to express succinctly that something is spoilt, or has gone bad in some way. Usually, when something is off, it's so far gone that you can detect it by smell alone. Indeed, tasting something that's off is often a very bad idea.

That the lobsters were off on this particular day was worse news than it would normally be. Normally, you could remove them from your menu for one night, or secure enough replacement lobsters to remedy the situation before your first customers arrived, and nobody would be the wiser.

But on the day in question, the lobsters were to be the main course of a private function we were cooking for: an international medical conference in Gerona, a beautiful city in northern Catalonia, near the French border. Dinner was to consist of four courses, what we called our Autumn Menu: a chestnut-cream-and-egg-white starter, hot pickled monkfish with spring onions and mushrooms, and a dessert of wild berries with vanilla cream. The *pièce de résistance* was a lobster dish garnished with a *cèpes* carpaccio and a salad with Parmesan and a pine-nut vinaigrette.

And there was another detail that made the lobster news particularly alarming. The dinner was to serve 3,200 people.

When chefs have nightmares, it's moments such as these that play out in our heads. Unfortunately, I was wide awake and the situation was very, very real.

A banquet for 3,200 people was not something I did every day. Never in my twenty-five years as a chef had I catered for anywhere close to such numbers. Our routine at El Bulli is fifty people a night. Admittedly, we serve 1,500 dishes at each sitting, but still, going from fifty to 3,200 is like jumping out of a warm, familiar bath into an icy hurricane sea.

Naturally, our kitchen at El Bulli wasn't up to the task. So, to ensure ample space, we commandeered three production centres:

two vast kitchens near by in Gerona and one in Barcelona. In addition, we hired plenty of extra help; more than 100 people were on the job. But even if we'd had 1,000 people on board, that wouldn't have prevented the lobsters from going bad.

I received the lobster call at 8 a.m. on 18 November 1995 – a date for ever imprinted in my memory – and was instantly plunged into a state of fear, uncertainty and panic the likes of which I have never experienced in my professional life, and hope never to experience again. The call came from the Barcelona kitchen, ironically situated in the city aquarium, right on the waterfront.

It wasn't just some of the lobster that was off; practically our entire stock had fermented overnight: 80 per cent of our lobster haul was unusable, inedible, unfit for human consumption – never mind in any state to grace a dish prepared by the chefs of what was then a two-star Michelin restaurant.

How could this have happened?

To maximise efficiency, we had shared out different tasks among the three production centres. The chief task of the aquarium team was to clean, boil and cut the lobster, before dispatching it to Gerona by road for assembly on the plate alongside the carpaccio and the salad. They had already done the cleaning and boiling and cutting – three pieces of lobster per dish – the night before, and the idea was that we'd simply load it all on to a van the next morning and off we'd go. Consequently, the lobster, all cut up and ready, had been placed inside white polystyrene containers until morning. We'd never done such a thing on such a scale and we supposed this was the right thing to do. The thermal containers insulated the lobster from the out-side temperature, which seemed like a perfectly good idea; indeed it *was* a good idea – at least for the drive north to

Gerona. When it came to the refrigerator, however, the night before, it was an absolute calamity. Inside the containers, the lobster pieces were also insulated from the cold of the refrigerator. And so, while we had carefully refrigerated the lobster, none of the cold could actually get through the polystyrene to reach the lobster – which consequently remained at room temperature all night. Room temperature, for that length of time, was the lobsters' ruin.

So, as you can see, it was the end of the world, the end of civilisation as we know it. My first reaction – which I imagine is the first reaction of anyone, in any context, on receiving catastrophic news – was, 'It's not possible. I cannot believe it. It can't be true. Tell me, please tell me it's a bad joke.' Once I had digested the indigestible and acknowledged that it was, indeed, true, that I was awake and so it was actually a lot worse than a nightmare, I proceeded to descend into despair. As second by mortifying second passed, the implications of what had happened sank in deeper: 3,200 mouths to feed in thirteen hours' time and the chief raw material of our main dish missing! I kept asking myself, What are we going to do? What the hell are we going to do? How in God's name are we going to manage now?

But then, with my heart still hammering at 100 kilometres an hour, I thought, OK, calm down. This is probably an absolutely hopeless case . . . but maybe there is something we can do, maybe we'll get lucky. Maybe there will be a miracle. So I started to think and think, trying to come up with ways to get round this. Though the one thing I knew for sure was that, whatever finally happened, ahead of me lay the most excruciatingly stressful day of my life.

The first and foremost question, of course, was how were we

going to find the 1,000 lobsters we needed – yes, 1,000 – in time to get them cleaned, cooked, delivered to Gerona (more than two hours away), and ready for consumption by nine o'clock that same night. So, amid the utter chaos of it all, I gave the order: 'Let's hunt down every last lobster in this city! Let's get them all until not one is left!' We got on the phone and called everyone and anyone who could possibly have a stock of fresh lobster. 'How many have you got? You've got fifteen? Great! Hold them, we'll go and collect them now . . . How many have you got? Twenty-five! Fantastic! Can you bring them over? Perfect.' After a frantic rush of phone calls, we assembled a team of ten people in the aquarium kitchen – most of them having imagined that their work had been over the day before – to clean, boil, and cut up the lobsters as they arrived.

By late morning, we realised that 500 lobsters was the maximum that we were going to get. So what to do? Simple. Here was the solution: reduce the contents of each dish by one piece of lobster, from three to two. That allowed us to stretch the utility of the 20 per cent that had not gone off overnight and to fill the quota we needed, especially as the happy news filtered down from Gerona around lunchtime – this did help bring the temperature down a bit, at last – that a few hundred participants of the medical conference would be going home early, and the total number of dishes required had fallen below the 3,000 mark.

By 11 a.m. we had our first batch ready, a hundred or so lobsters' worth. Off went the first vanload to Gerona. There was some slight relief at its departure, but it was mostly overshadowed by the suspense, the worry, that the van might break down or crash or God knows what. In those days, we didn't have mobile phones. You couldn't keep track of the van's progress the way you could now. So what happened was that the van driver, under strict orders to reassure us, would phone us at intervals – the team in Barcelona *and* the two kitchens in Gerona – from a motorway café or petrol station to let us know that he was making progress, that he was edging his way up to his destination. 'It's OK. All's well. I'm on my way. Relax, guys!' We would all cheer with relief. But between calls, it was hell. After what had happened, we were preconditioned for disaster. If anything could go wrong, we imagined, it would.

And yet, miraculously, it didn't. Five vanloads of chopped lobster successfully made it from the Barcelona aquarium to Gerona – each time inspiring the same drama of anxiety and reassuring phone calls – and finally, at about six in the evening, we looked at the dish, reduced to two pieces of lobster but beefed up with an extra helping of *cèpes* carpaccio, and knew that, barring the habitual worries that always loom for a chef at this time of night, the immediate crisis was over. We had survived.

And, in the end, I learnt some lessons from all this. First, never store things that need to be cold inside a fridge in closed polystyrene containers. Second, keep a closer eye on things, especially when you have so much to do in so little time, when your available reaction time, in case things go wrong, is drastically reduced. When you're feeding up to 200 people there's a certain amount of flexibility built in, some room to manoeuvre. More than 200 and you're in a totally new space. The logistical dimension of the exercise becomes so much more unwieldy.

The final and most valuable lesson I learnt is that every day you start fresh. I know it sounds trite, maybe even foolish, but it's true. Every day is a new challenge, a new adventure, and you must never be complacent. You must be constantly on your toes, ready to deal with the unexpected, ready to respond – with as cool a head as you can – to whatever surprise comes.

(*Translated from the Spanish and co-written with John Carlin*)

What do you eat for breakfast?
Fruit.

What dish would you cook in order to seduce someone?
The 'tasting' menu on the terrace at El Bulli.

What do you never cook?
Animals that are not normally part of our eating culture.

What's the one dish you find hard to get right?
Hot ice cream.

Our First Friday

NEIL PERRY

Neil Perry opened Sydney's Rockpool restaurant in 1989 with his business partner and cousin Trish Richards. He is the author of Rockpool *and* Simply Asian, *and is working on a third book and four recipe CDs. He is also a television presenter on the LifeStyle Channel. Before Rockpool, Perry worked at Sails restaurant at McMahons Point and in Rose Bay, then became head chef at Barrenjoey Restaurant in Palm Beach and Perry's in Paddington. In October 1986, he opened the Blue Water Grill at Bondi Beach. Rockpool won the* Sydney Morning Herald Good Food Guide's *Restaurant of the Year 2004 award and is ranked one of the Top Fifty restaurants in the world by* Restaurant *magazine in Britain.*

OPENING A NEW restaurant is a stressful business. It doesn't matter how many times you've done it, how much you plan, or how many experts you surround yourself with, there will always be surprises waiting around every corner.

Some surprises aren't really surprises, because you learn to expect them: it's likely that one cook or another will quit at a highly inconvenient time, often the week of your launch; some piece of kitchen equipment will give you trouble, either because it doesn't function properly or because it's an unfamiliar model and there's a struggle to master it; and your opening day will be rescheduled at least three times.

But there are certain surprises you simply can't anticipate, no matter how active and boundless your imagination. The debut week of my restaurant Rockpool, sixteen years ago in Sydney, was proof positive of this statement. In addition to the intensity of construction, dining-room design, menu-planning, hiring and training, once we opened, we were faced with the daily drama of getting the place up and running for lunch, then shutting down, going through a whole new round of prep, and reopening for dinner.

For kitchen professionals, doing lunch and dinner is like cramming two work days into one calendar day. It was very hectic and difficult, an extreme test of physical and mental stamina, not just for me but also for my crew of twelve cooks, all of whom worked both shifts back to back. If you were there in the morning, you were there when the restaurant closed after midnight.

A nice break in the day – the eye of the storm, so to speak – was our nightly staff dinner, served about thirty minutes before the first customers arrived each evening.

Some restaurants are pretty cheap when it comes to their staff meal; they feed their employees the lowliest of ingredients and expect them to shovel it down in seconds, then get right back to work. But at Rockpool, our staff meals were done in the proper spirit, a gesture of thanks for everyone's hard work and a chance for the men to have some shared leisure time in the midst of a gruelling schedule.

On our first Friday night, we were going to have lamb chops for staff dinner. One of the guys was barbecuing the chops on our indoor grill, and as the char-tinged smoke wafted through the kitchen, our hunger pangs spiked. We had been around food all day, but this was to be *our* food, and it was at this moment that our professional indifference to all the delicious temptations before us finally gave way. We paced around with ravenous, impatient grins on our faces, tortured by the tantalising smell of the chops, eager to dig in to a richly deserved feast.

I was deep in this heightened, near-excruciating state of anticipation when all of a sudden I felt a spray of icy water in my face, a forceful, unending blast shocking in its temperature, its magnitude – its very existence. Where on earth was it coming from?

Shaking my head, trying in vain to avoid the rush, I looked round to see that all of the guys were being hosed down as well. Water was catching them right in the face. Some were ducking or cowering to protect themselves, others were defiantly squinting into the gush to determine its source.

I was stunned. We all were. What in the world was happening? Had a pipe burst in the ceiling? *Were* there even pipes in the ceiling?

Finally, I realised what had happened: lamb chops are fatty things, and the fat dripping into the flames of the barbecue had caused some pretty big flare-ups. Those flare-ups, in turn, had set off the sprinkler system. It was only at that moment that I noticed there was a fire alarm going off as well.

I don't know if you've ever experienced the deluge created by an industrial sprinkler system, but it is unforgettable. It dumps what feels like 30,000 litres of water per second, and it covers a pretty fair whack of territory, dispersing it in all directions.

The effect was like being on a leaky submarine, with water pouring down on us without end. And the water got *everywhere*. It soaked our clothes, it collected on the counters and ruined all the *place* (short for *mise en place* – the prepared ingredients at each station), it pooled up on the floor, it flowed under the doors. It was absolute chaos, and there was nothing we could do but watch.

Soon enough, the alarm was drowned out by the sound of approaching sirens. The fire brigade raced on to the scene with three trucks, and a small army of men rushed through the door, ready to put out any blaze in their path. More hoses – just what we needed.

Once the situation became clear, the firemen turned off the alarm and the sprinklers and returned peace and quiet to our soggy kitchen. We explained about the lamb chops and they kindly laughed it off; I think they must respond to food-triggered alarms all the time.

It was their captain who told me what our problem was: sprinkler systems are set to go off when heat-sensitive tubing inside turns a certain colour. Most restaurants have tubing with a relatively high resistance, but our contractor had made a mistake and used the conventional type. It was a miracle, really, that the alarm hadn't gone off on our first night.

With the sprinklers switched off and the fire engines headed back to the station, we turned our attention to trying to salvage our evening. Our first guests would be showing up at any minute . . .

We spent the next twenty minutes just getting the water out – mopping up the counters with kitchen towels, pushing the water from the floor out the back door with brooms and mops, and throwing away the *place* that was destroyed.

Then we ran off to the lockers to change into whatever extra clothes we had so we could be as dry as possible that night. One thing none of us had was extra shoes, so it was a very squeaky couple of hours in the kitchen.

Yet somehow we made it through the evening. We had to take a few items off the menu – for example, the deep-fryer was full of water and we couldn't get it to turn on, so any fried preparations were removed. Other dishes were prepared as you would prepare them at home – completely made to order, with the cook doing all the chopping and slicing he normally would have completed before staff meal.

Amazingly, even though we have an open kitchen at Rockpool, the customers had no idea that anything disastrous had happened, which is a real tribute to my opening team.

After service that night, I took the men out for about 400 beers. We probably consumed as much liquid as had poured down on us earlier in the evening, and we had earned every precious drop.

What do you eat for breakfast?
Fresh juice that reflects the season, Bircher muesli.

What dish would you cook in order to seduce someone?
Toast with caviar, and champagne.

What do you never cook?
Kiwi fruit. I hate it.

What's the one dish you find hard to get right?
The next one I'm working on for the restaurant, as it has to be perfect before it goes out.

A Secret Worth Keeping
TESSA KIROS

Tessa Kiros was born in London to a Finnish mother and Greek-Cypriot father. She moved to South Africa at the age of four, and after completing her schooling at the age of eighteen, devoted herself to living, working, and learning about food around the world. This mission took her to the Groucho Club in London, a French chef's restaurant in Athens, Australia and Mexico. It also led her to her current home of Tuscany, where she lives with her husband and two daughters. Kiros's books include Twelve, *a chronicle of 'what Tuscans eat, and when', and* Falling Cloudberries, *which gathers her favourite memories and recipes from the countries she has visited and lived in.*

F OR ANYONE WHO loves to cook, it can be a challenge to contain the enthusiasm and excitement whipped up by planning a special meal. Writers are often counselled to keep their ideas to themselves until they have a draft to share – because it's never yours to control once you've given it voice –

and I'd offer cooks very similar advice: until you're ready to present your plates to the table, keep your plans to yourself.

Two formative incidents have inspired this personal policy, and both were intensified by their settings – charming, romantic, and *remote*.

The first occurred years ago when I was the caterer for a film company in South Africa. This was a job full of unique challenges. Every day, the number of people for whom I was cooking changed. I was told how many in the morning, then I would prepare the food in my kitchen. When the call came that it was lunchtime on the set, which could be in a faraway location, like the desert, I'd have to stop cooking, cram all the food into containers, and jump into a van that would take me to the production.

On one particular day, I was charged with preparing lunch for twenty-five people. For dessert, I had two cheesecakes in the oven, one on the top rack and one on the bottom. When I was alerted that it was time to leave, I opened the oven door, only to discover that the surface of the cheesecake on the upper rack was badly burnt. With no time to spare, I nevertheless packed it up, along with the properly cooked cheesecake, and got in the van.

As I hurtled along towards the set, I imagined the frowning faces with which the burnt cheesecake would be met. But what could I do? My schedule didn't offer any contingency time, and once I was deposited at my destination, there was nothing in sight but sand, sand, and more sand, unless you counted the horizon.

And, yet, not telling anybody of my impending embarrassment proved to be prudent. Against all odds, as the crew were eating, I noticed an abandoned carton of ready-made custard.

Without hesitation, not even to wonder whose it was or to thank my lucky stars for this bit of good fortune, I commandeered it, spreading the custard over the top of the burnt cheesecake.

When the crew members began to ask, 'What's for dessert?' I said, 'Well, over here is a cheesecake.' Then, pointing to the custard-covered one, I bravely announced, 'And here we have a caramelised cheesecake with French vanilla icing.'

Sure enough, the caramelised cheesecake went first, the lesson being that, when something goes wrong, don't announce it. Instead, throw your shoulders back and confidently attach some creative adjectives to the dish in question.

The other relevant incident took place at my home in Tuscany between Florence and Siena. Autumn was beginning to wrap the region in its dark, romantic shroud, and I was in the mood for a white-truffle dinner. I invited some friends over, telling them all to expect just that.

I procured the necessary ingredients – at some expense, I might add – and had the meal all prepared and ready to be finished and served. The five courses included a *crostino* topped with cheese, *rucola* (rocket), a sliver of truffle and a drop of olive oil; a pasta with truffles and butter; and a chicken breast with truffles slipped under the skin, accompanied by a simple salad.

My guests arrived on the designated night, and I welcomed them all with some *prosecco*.

After chatting to them for a while, I invited them to be seated at the dinner table, and stepped round into my open kitchen, in full view of my friends, to begin plating the dishes. Their anticipation was palpable, and rightly so, for who doesn't love the thought of a truffle dinner?

As I prepared the *crostini*, layering the ingredients on top of the bread slices, I took a truffle slicer in one hand and a truffle in the other. I shaved a sliver on to one *crostino*, then another, then another . . . and then happened upon the worst possible discovery: the truffle was infested with worms. The little thread-like invaders had made a nest of this most prized foodstuff and were squirming within it.

For a moment, I entertained the notion of slicing only the perimeter of the truffles, but quickly realised that that would never produce enough for the five courses I had planned.

Just as was the case with that cheesecake, I was utterly without recourse. I had no extra truffles, not even some preserved ones, it was too late in the year to turn to my garden for help, the closest market was twenty kilometres away, and my friends had driven from distances that far, or further, so could not help by raiding their own pantries.

I can safely say, without irony, that there was a better chance of shooting a wild boar in the surrounding countryside than there was of finding a more conventional solution to my predicament.

I did the only thing I could, and served my friends the truffle dinner minus the truffles. There was the *crostino*. There was pasta *in bianco*, or 'white pasta' tossed with cheese and butter – a dish so notoriously bland that in Italy it's traditionally served to sick children. And there was very plain roast chicken. I can't remember the fourth course, or the dessert, no doubt because I've blacked out some details of this disappointing affair.

And yet, while not special, the meal would have been perfectly fine had my guests not been expecting five courses punctuated by the most glorious and fabled food in all of Italy.

So, do yourself a favour when cooking for friends and family: keep the meal a secret until the moment of service is at hand, and if something goes wrong, don't hide it, *celebrate* it, as though it was what you had in mind from the start.

What do you eat for breakfast?
Nothing or anything. Café latte and croissants (French, crisp, flaky and buttery). One of the things I love about living in Italy is the coffee. It's beautiful everywhere.

What dish would you cook in order to seduce someone?
Prawns with feta, lemon, chilli and garlic.

What do you never cook?
Bubble and squeak. I have never cooked it but have heard it mentioned various times so I may try, as it sounds happy and fun.

What's the one dish you find hard to get right?
Boiled eggs exactly the same way every time. Some ethnic foods very different from mine, e.g., Thai and Chinese – because ingredients and grannies to learn from are hard to come by (will somebody please open a Thai restaurant in Florence?).

A Christmas Story
BILL GRANGER

*Born in Melbourne, Australia, Bill Granger moved to Sydney
when he was nineteen. As an art student with a passion for
food, he worked as a waiter and his focus gradually shifted
from art to food. In time, he opened his own restaurants,
bills (sic) in 1993 in the Sydney suburb of Darlinghurst, and
a second bills in the nearby suburb of Surry Hills in 1996. In
2005, he opened bills Woollahra. In 2003, Bill Granger
became consultant to the Lifestore retail concept for Marks
& Spencer in the UK. He makes frequent appearances on
television, and has his own series,* bills food, *on the Life
Style Channel in Australia. His books include* bills Sydney
Food, bills food, bills open kitchen, *and, most recently,*
Simply Bill.*

I'LL BE HONEST: when I first opened my restaurant, bills,
in 1993, I was a well-meaning amateur. I had never worked
in other people's restaurants, and was a little bit ditzy, prone to

the kind of errors one simply doesn't make in more polished establishments.

What can I tell you? I was eager to get on with it, to start cooking and serving my food and offering the kind of hospitality I'd had in mind for a long time. As a consequence, I learnt a lot of my craft and my profession on the job, and it's gone, for the most part, very well. But in the early days, before I had seasoned professionals to help me along, we lived by the skin of our teeth. Every day there was the added drama of financial pressure and the question of how we'd fare in the long run. We were grateful for every bit of good news, every positive notice in the papers, and any meaningful attention that was thrown our way.

All of our customers were dear to us, but because of all these behind-the-scenes factors, there was one early fan who meant a great deal, an editor of *Harper's Bazaar*. She was a really great woman, and a very important customer, because she liked our little café so much that she ate breakfast there every single day of the week.

In a burst of generosity, towards the end of 1993, this editor asked me if I'd like to cater for the annual *Harper's* Christmas party on a Friday afternoon in December. For a young chef and restaurateur, moments like these are the kind of thing you work for and which keep you going – you take them as a sign that you're doing something right and that the word will get out and you'll be sustained in your labour of love. So I was delighted, not only because the party would expose us to other influential editors at the magazine, as well as advertisers and people who frequently dine out, but also because – on a strictly practical level – it would be a welcome infusion of cash.

The party was to host about forty-five people at Darling Park, a secluded, harbourside area that in location and spirit suggested a secret garden. We conceived the party after the fashion of a Tuscan feast – there would be a big trellised table groaning with a variety of *antipasti*-style food, and waiters pouring champagne – the perfect way to celebrate the Christmas season which, of course, in Australia takes place in the summer.

Because we didn't have a separate catering kitchen, my cooks and I prepared all the food after dinner service Thursday night and on into the wee hours of Friday morning. Come mid-morning Friday, I got into a van along with three waiters, three cooks and the food we'd been fussing over all night. We arrived at the park and set up the table under a frangipani tree.

The food looked lovely: there was poached salmon and asparagus salad with watercress mayonnaise, chicken and pistachio salad, prawn sandwiches, mango trifles, and so it went on. The display was, I was sure, all our hosts could have hoped for, suggesting generosity, good taste, and pure uncomplicated pleasure.

The lunch was to begin at one o'clock, but as the hour arrived I couldn't help but notice that nobody, not even my editor friend, had arrived. There was no sound of approaching cars or car doors slamming; there were no voices wafting through the trees. Well, I thought, as the time crawled to ten past one. It must be the madness of Christmas: everyone must be stuck at the office, or in traffic.

At half-past one, I couldn't disguise my concern, pacing about and trying not to meet the gaze of my comrades, who had a look on their faces that said, unmistakably, Something's wrong. Come twenty to two, I was beside myself. What could possibly have happened to everyone?

I called the editor at her office, trying to sound as casual as possible.

'Hi, Bill. How are you?'

I put on my best relaxed voice. 'Fine, fine, thanks.'

'You know, we're all so looking forward to the party next Friday.'

Next Friday?

I wanted to smack myself on the forehead. This is why chefs have assistants, managers, and the like. We're meant to cook, not coordinate. The wrong Friday! Of all the ridiculous . . .

I managed to get control of myself and quickly adjust. 'I'm looking forward to it, too, thanks. Just wanted to make sure we were all set.'

'Oh, we can't wait.'

'Oh, neither can we,' I said, gazing around at all the food that proved the truth of my comment beyond a doubt.

We said our goodbyes and I hung up, never letting on that I was phoning her from the park or that the party was all set to go that instant.

What, I wonder, would you have done at a moment like that?

We could have lugged all the food back to the restaurant and maybe put it on as a special that night, or the next day, or offered it up for staff meal over the next few days.

But I have to say, I've always had a sense of humour about these things, so I instructed my cooks and waiters – friends of mine all – to call their friends and invite them to join us in this beautiful harbourside setting.

Before too long, we would at last hear the distant slamming of car doors, the drifting voices of approaching revellers, the ecstatic hellos as they arrived on the scene. Oh, sure – they were our friends, not the VIP guests we were expecting, but we had one hell of a party nonetheless. The staff mixed in with the guests and everyone helped themselves to food and wine until the table was picked clean and the last drop had been drained from the last bottle.

It was an afternoon to remember, to be sure.

It also made the official party better the next week. We learnt little lessons from that afternoon, like discovering better ways to pack up the food. The following Friday, we also brought along blankets for the impromptu picnics that we now knew would break out on the lawn . . . because we'd been sitting there on the grass ourselves and wishing there was something soft between us and the hard ground!

Today, with the benefit of a dozen years' experience, cooking for forty would hardly be more of a strain than cooking at home, but at the time mixing up my Fridays was a blessing in disguise, not to mention a welcome Christmas present and fond memory for the friends who joined us on that sunny December afternoon.

What do you eat for breakfast?
Usually an egg on toast, or cheese and tomato on toast, or tahini and tomato on toast, or some gravlax and a squeeze of lemon juice on toast.

What dish would you cook in order to seduce someone?
Anything that goes with champagne.

What do you never cook?
I'm not a big fan of offal.

What's the one dish you find hard to get right?
I'm usually pretty good at most things if I give myself the time.
I'm pretty stubborn and I'll work hard to get it right: practice
fixes most things for me in the kitchen.

Kitchen Basics
DAVID THOMPSON

David Thompson was born in 1960 in Sydney, Australia. In 1986 he travelled to Thailand and instantly became enamoured of the country, its people and its culture. A year later he moved to Bangkok. In 1991 David returned to Sydney to open his first restaurant, the Darley Street Thai, which the Sydney Morning Herald *voted 'Best Thai Restaurant' for the next eight years. In July 2001, he opened Nahm in London. In 2002 Nahm became the first Thai restaurant to be awarded a Michelin star, which it has kept. In 2003 David was voted Outstanding London Chef at the Tio Pepe ITV restaurant awards. He has also written the most comprehensive guide available to authentic Thai cookery,* Thai Food. *Published in late 2001, it has won many awards, including the André Simon Book of the Year, the Glenfiddich Cookery Book of the Year, and a James Beard award in the US. David divides his time between London, Bangkok and Sydney.*

T HERE ARE MANY unspoken rules in a kitchen that really should be followed. And I am going to tell you about a few important ones that I once forgot.

It all began with an unexpected phone call asking me to cook for a charity . . . a gallery . . . a dinner . . . a good cause . . . it all sounded so easy, so right, and nothing needed to be done immediately. It was brilliant timing when I think back; the event was several months away and, like almost any cook, I'll agree to anything if it's so distant, especially in the middle of a busy day when I'm prepared to do just about anything to get off the phone. So I blithely agreed to the proposal.

A few days later the arrangements were confirmed. She said the organisers would do everything – hire the venue, arrange suppliers for the food, and even enlist trained staff both in the kitchen and on the floor. It was to be in a venerable building near the Mall. Its atmosphere was fantastic, she said, made more beautiful by the most wonderful paintings hanging on its ornate walls. There was no need to see the venue now – I could see it in a few months, much closer to the date.

Maybe it's a cook thing, but when things are not in front of me I tend to forget about them promptly, and so as time passed the whole prospect receded nicely. But then a phone call made it all come rushing back and I was invited to go and have a look at the gallery. It was, as promised, lovely. It was impressive. It seemed perfect.

I asked to see the kitchen as we walked down a long, dark, dingy corridor, and was led into an empty space. When I asked where the kitchen was, with a smile the organisers shot back, 'You're standing in it!' I returned the smile weakly, as I slumped against a wall. I really couldn't speak. There was no equipment, no stoves, no hood, no nothing – not even running water, just the four bare walls! Well, not quite bare as they too had their paintings – they would have to go, I thought.

I bleakly contemplated the prospects. When I was finally able to voice my fears, I was told not to worry, a kitchen would be set up with everything I needed. Fair enough, I thought, after all, that's what some caterers contend with every day. Surely we could cope with a temporary portable kitchen for one night. It would take careful planning, however, to make sure the menu suited the circumstances. Clearly most of the food would have to be prepared in advance with as little cooking in the 'kitchen' as possible. Some swordfish braised with star anise and celery, a sweet-and-sour curry of duck with cardamom, peanuts and shallots was in order . . . and perhaps some yellow-bean relish with prawns and white turmeric and a salad of crab meat, mint, lemongrass and Thai basil with a vengeful amount of chillies. A smile came back to my face.

As the day of the event drew near, we prepared the meal and were assisted by some volunteers from a nearby catering college – the organisation's charity extended to giving a few young culinary criminals the opportunity to see how they fared along-side some professionals. They picked up a few tips and we worked up a storm. In fact, my fears for the night were beginning to subside as we managed to finish in good time, just before the van arrived to take the food to the gallery.

When the van came to a stop, to my surprise, a jaunty woman jumped out and beamed widely. She said what a wonderful night it would be as she rubbed her hands together. We loaded up the van and she hopped into the driver's seat, waved us a cherry farewell, and started off . . . only to stop suddenly as she hit the wall. Giggling, she reversed with equal bonhomie only to slam into the other wall, and moving backwards and forwards managed to wedge the van solidly in the alleyway. Every attempt to dislodge the van merely meant it became more firmly jammed as it scraped against the red brick of the buildings. For the next hour and a half, a growing number of cooks, apprentices, and laughing passers-by surrounded the van, giving instructions on how to turn the wheel this way and that to dislodge the vehicle. I lost my voice from shouting what to do and where to go. 'At least the salad will be tossed,' said one assistant. I could only stare at the little crook – and then I hit him.

Quickly leaving the scene, we flagged a taxi and went straight to the venue. At least I could start to work there, I reasoned. We walked through the dining room, which looked splendid, and into the kitchen only to discover . . . nothing! The room was as dingy and barren as before. No equipment had arrived; it was on its way but it was stuck somewhere. I knew exactly what they meant. Don't worry, they said, it would be there soon and it would be set up quickly. Just then my mobile rang telling me that the van would be there soon, having finally found its way out with the help of the police who apparently arrived just after I left. I said there was no need to hurry as we didn't have a kitchen. The line went dead . . . but soon the van came swerving up the Mall and screeched to a stop in front of the gallery with an unsettling thud. Everyone looked round but nobody dared say anything! But I know what they were thinking: dinner was served. I glowered at them and their distasteful wit.

While everything was being unpacked, I did the professional thing and turned to the bottle. I had a drink, a very manly and very welcome gin. It was so good, so calming, and so medicinal, that I just had to have another. No one commented, in fact they poured it for me. I think it almost brought a smile to my face.

And just as I was about to beg for another drink the kitchen arrived.

We struggled to carry in the equipment. Ovens, hot tops, fridges, and preparation tables – we had to lug them in. I must say the kitchen was set up with surprising speed. But when we tried to turn on the equipment, there was a crackling, a bang, and we were plunged into darkness. The lights returned when the concierge came down to see what the screaming was about. 'I thought someone was being murdered,' he said. Not quite yet, I thought, not quite yet. Beautiful old buildings can only be admired for their beauty, not always for their practicalities, and our old girl couldn't take the strain that all the electrical equipment placed upon her system. She swooned – and I almost did too. With an irritating smile the old gent explained that we couldn't possibly use all this equipment at once. Perhaps the system could contend with a little at a time.

We finally found a way to operate. Not only did I have to call the service, that is, direct where the food was to go, but I also controlled the power, deciding who had the juice and who didn't. This I did arbitrarily, perhaps even punitively. Some sections had light, others stewed, a few fried, while those who laughed too much at the absurdity of it all were left in the dark – after all, they had so little to do as their salad was already tossed!

Somehow we managed to pull it together. As the guests arrived, we served the canapés with the champagne. The guests were unaware of the dizzy state of the cooks and their fraught preparations. We managed to snatch the dinner from the jaws of disaster. I put it down to the gin and perhaps the hard work of everybody else when faced with such dark circumstances. By the end of it I was utterly exhausted. Calling the pass as well as holding the reins had taken its toll. I smiled weakly as I took my leave and my wracked body home.

We met to debrief a week later. The organisers said how wonderful the night had been and I smiled through gritted teeth. They said it was such a success they wanted to do it again. *Again*, I thought. *Again*?

I fumed silently, Not bloody likely . . . after what I'd been put through . . . no kitchen . . . no electricity . . . and certainly not enough gin . . . The three basics of any well-run kitchen. Never. I thought, never again would I break this unspoken rule.

They poured me a drink and as we clinked glasses, I said, 'Sure.' They were as surprised as I was. Shocked, I sank back in the chair with a frozen smile and stared at the walls . . . after all, it was at least a year away.

What do you eat for breakfast?
As little as possible.

What dish would you cook in order to seduce someone?
Champagne.

What do you never cook?
Anything that moves.

What's the one dish you find hard to get right?
My life!

New Year's Meltdown
ANTHONY BOURDAIN

Anthony Bourdain has been a chef for nearly three decades, and in 2000 he chronicled that experience in Kitchen Confidential, *which has been translated into twenty-four languages, leading him to the conclusion that 'chefs are the same everywhere'. He is the executive chef at Brasserie Les Halles in New York City.*

IN MY LONG and chequered career I have been witness to, party to, and even singularly responsible for any number of screwups, missteps, and overreaches. I am not Alain Ducasse. The focus of my career has not always been a relentless drive towards excellence. As a mostly journeyman chef, knocking around the restaurant business for twenty-eight years, I've witnessed some pretty ugly episodes of culinary disaster. I have seen an accidentally glass-laden breaded veal cutlet cause a customer to rise up in the middle of a crowded dining room and begin keening and screaming with pain as blood dribbled from his mouth. I've watched restaurants endure mid-dinner-rush fires, floods, and rodent infiltration – as well as the more innocuous annoyances of used Band-Aids, tufts of hair, and industrial staples showing up in the niçoise salad. Busboy stabbing busboy, customer beating up customer, waiters duking it out on the dining-room floor – I've seen it all. But never have I seen such a shameful synergy of Truly Awful Things happen, and in such spectacular fashion, as on New Year's Eve 1991, a date that surely deserves to live in New York restaurant infamy. It was the all-time, award-winning, jumbo-sized restaurant train wreck, a night where absolutely everything went wrong that could go wrong, where the greatest number of people got hurt, and an entire kitchen bowed its head in shame and fear – while outside the kitchen doors, waiters trembled at the slaughter-house their once hushed and elegant dining room had become.

Like Operation Market Garden (the ill-fated Allied invasion of the Netherlands) or Stalingrad – or the musicals of Andrew Lloyd Webber – responsibility for the disaster that followed rests, ultimately, with one man. In this case it was a talented and resourceful chef we'll call Bobby Thomas. Bobby had the idea that he could create an ambitious menu – as good as his always excellent à la carte menus – and serve it to the 350 people who would be filling the nightclub/restaurant we'll call NiteKlub. He also felt confident enough in his abilities that he could pretty much wait until the last minute to put the whole thing together: little details like telling his staff what the fuck they were going to be serving, and how. In his visionary wisdom, Bobby did not share his thinking or his plans with others. Like the strategic brainiacs who thought invading Russia to be a good idea, he was undisturbed by useful details ('Mein Fuhrer? Are you aware winter is coming?'). Those who might have pointed out the obvious warning signs were not included in Bobby's conceptualising of what could well have been a spectacular success – for a dinner party of twenty. Bobby was, after all, a kind of a genius. And it's often the geniuses who put us in a world of pain.

I arrived at NiteKlub at about a half-hour before the shift, the other cooks trickling in after me. We pulled on our whites, cranked up the radio, and, as usual, stood around waiting for someone to tell us what to do. Our leader had characteristically neglected to entrust us with a prep list. So we did what cooks left unbriefed and unsupervised tend to do, which was stand around gossiping.

The lobsters arrived first. There were cases of them, so many that they reached to the ceiling, 125 of the things, skittering around under wet newspaper and heaps of crushed ice. Since I was *de facto* quartermaster, and the guy who signed for such things, the cooks – Frankie Five Angels, Matt, Orlando, Steven, Dougie, Adam Real Last Name Unknown, and Dog Boy – all stood there expectantly, looking at me, waiting for instructions as a puddle of water grew larger and larger from the rapidly melting ice. What do we do with them? Who knows? Bobby hadn't left a prep list. Do we blanch them? Cook them all the way? Whack 'em into wriggling chunks? Shuck them, split them, or turn the damn things into bisque? We don't know. 'Cause Bobby hasn't left a menu.

The poultry arrived next. Boned-out *poussin*, duck breasts, bones, a case of foie gras. We cleaned up the duck breasts nicely, put on stock with the bones (that didn't take much to surmise), and laid out the *poussins* on sheet pans and got everything in the walk-in for when Bobby showed. We wanted to start in on the case of foie gras – whole loaves of the stuff! – but were we making terrine, which would require us to open them up and start yanking out veins, or were we leaving them whole for pan-searing? We didn't know. And once you tear open a liver, you can't untear it. So we left those alone. When the meat order arrived, we cleaned up the tenderloins, but left them whole, not having any idea of portion size, whether we were making filet mignon or tournedos or Chateaubriand or beef fucking Wellington for that matter.

Oysters! There was a collective moan from the team, as not even a madman would want to put oysters on a menu for over 300. Perhaps we could crack them open ahead of time. But should we? What if . . . what *if* Bobby had planned oysters on the half-shell? In which case I'd be cracking oysters to order all night, since the customers, for the $275 per person they were paying, would prefer them moist and fresh. It was too horrible to contemplate. Out of the corner of my eye I saw Steven peel off out the back door – which meant he was probably going to score – and from the way Frankie was working his jaw muscles, half the cooks were well into the coke already and likely looking for a re-up.

When the produce order came in, it was getting towards panic time. Two cases of oranges, a case of lemons, ten cases of *mâche* (lamb's lettuce) – which, at least, we could clean – Belgian endive, fennel, wild mushrooms, the ubiquitous baby zucchinis, yellow squashes, and pattypan squash and baby carrots that Bobby so loved. Dry goods followed, an impenetrable heap of long-haul purchases: fryer oil, salad oil, vinegar, flour, canned goods. There was no way of knowing what was for today and what was for next week.

We peeled the carrots. It was two o'clock now, cocaine and indecision grinding the heart right out of the afternoon. And still no Bobby.

Truffles arrived. Nice. Then the fish. Not so nice because it was Dover sole – a bitch to clean and an even bigger bitch to cook in large numbers. Orlando, Frankie, and I got down on the sole with rubber gloves and kitchen shears, trimming off the spines. Matt and Dougie cut chive sticks and plucked chervil tops and basil flowers and made *gaufrette* potatoes for garnish, because we knew – if we knew anything – that we'd be using a lot of those. Dog Boy was relegated to fiddling with the dial on the radio. A new hire, Dog Boy was a skateboarder with a recently pierced tongue and absolutely useless for anything – he could fuck up a wet dream – so it was best that he was kept safely out of the way. Adam, at least, knew we'd need bread, so he stayed reasonably busy balling dough and putting loaves in the oven – which was ironic, really, as Adam was usually the last person to know what was going on about anything, and here he was, currently the best-informed person in the kitchen.

By four o'clock, with still no evidence of Bobby and no word, the mood was turning ugly. Dougie's neck and cheeks were red, which meant he'd been hitting the sauce somewhere. Frankie was retelling, for the umpteenth time, the story of how he had communicated the plot to *Cliffhanger* to Sylvester Stallone during a three-second near-telepathic encounter by the men's room of Planet Hollywood, his previous employer. He'd as good as written that movie! – despite the fact that he couldn't even pronounce it, calling it '*Clifthangah*' – and one of these days, he'd get paid for it. That's if Sly's 'people' didn't 'get to him first'. Frankie, while high on blow, was often under the impression that various 'agents of Stallone' were 'watching him' as he clearly 'knew too much'. When we all started laughing (and how could we not?) the by now manically high, dangerously paranoid Frankie began to tweak. This was not good. As Frankie was taller and bigger and stronger than all of us (over six foot six) and a vicious hockey player sensitive to criticism, things could get really crazy.

'Fucking Bobby,' muttered Dougie again. Dougie, at least, wouldn't get violent. He was more of a sulker. But he might very well just disappear if discouraged. He'd done it before – just walked out the door and disappeared for a few days.

I nervously looked at the clock and debated doing exactly that myself. Happily, when I looked back, Matt was doing his pitch-perfect Frankie Pentangeli imitation from *The Godfather II*: 'Oh . . . sure, Senator . . . sure . . . that Michael Corleone . . . Michael Corleone did this . . . Michael Corleone did that,' which always gave Frankie the giggles. Violence, for now anyway, seemed to have been averted.

Time passed. We continued to set up as best we could. At five-thirty, Bobby finally rolled in. I say rolled in because he was (not unusually) on Rollerblades, wearing a new *Blues Traveler* tour jacket he'd scored off a private client and that charming little-boy smile that had so successfully helped convince a legion of hostesses and floor staff to come into close contact with Bobby's genitals. We, however, were not so charmed.

'Uh . . . Bobby? What's the menu?' I said. 'We'd really kind of like to know.'

Bobby just smiled, gave us the Ronnie James Dio 'devil horn' hand sign, skated back to his office, and emerged a few moments later in his whites, bearing the fatal document:

The NiteKlub New Year's Eve Menu 1992

Oysters Baked in Champagne Sauce with Beluga Caviar

or

Pan-Seared Foie Gras with Apricot Chutney

Port Wine Sauce, and Toasted Brioche

or

Beggar's Purses of Diver Scallops and Wild Mushrooms

or

Truffle Soup

followed by
Dover Sole with Citrus Beurre
Lobster in a Shellfish Nage with Fennel
Chestnut-and-truffle-stuffed *Poussin* with Foie Gras Sauce
Chateaubriand 'Rossini' with Baby Vegetables
and Chive Mashed Potatoes

followed by
Harlequin Soufflé
New Year's Parfait
Lemon Tart
Profiteroles

To be honest, my memory is not perfect on the exact menu choices. I approximate. What *is* burnt permanently into my brain, however, is the simple fact that this was a killer menu to do *à la minute* and seemed heavily skewed towards the sauté station. Which was not, tactically or strategically, our strongest point. The hot app station appeared overladen with dishes as well, and as Frankie Five Angels was already, at this early hour, quietly having an amusing conversation with himself, the prospects of a smooth night in that area seemed . . . unlikely. Our fearless leader, though, brimmed with insouciance that we took for confidence. My muttered concerns were dismissed – understandably, given my pessimistic nature, and my kitchen nickname of the time: 'Dr Doom'.

Bobby curtly gave us our prep assignments and a brief run-down of how he expected us to prepare and present his crea-tions. To our credit, we quickly put our stations together, set up our *mise en place*, dug in, and by seven we were loaded and ready for the first orders.

It should be pointed out that I had, basically, nothing to do but crack oysters – which I sensibly did in advance (given they were to be baked) – and help Adam plate desserts. Everything else was coming off hot appetiser (Frankie and Dougie), grill (Matt), or sauté (Steven and Orlando). Dog Boy was sent home after a less-than-gruelling half-day.

Half an hour later, there were still no tickets. The little printer hooked up to the waiters' computer-order systems lay silent. Our two runners, Manuel and Ed, informed us that the guests were arriving, the dining room filling, and all of us hoped that they'd start getting the orders in fast, in comfortably staggered fashion, so we could set a nice pace without getting swamped all at once.

'Tell them to get those orders in,' snarled Bobby. 'Let's knock down some early tables! C'mon!'

But nothing happened. A half-hour passed, then an hour, as our now-full house of New Year's revellers sat at their tables, admired each other's clothes, drank Veuve Clicquot, and pre-sumably pondered their menus. It would be a long night.

The first order came in at eight-thirty. *Clack clack clack* . . . *dit dit dit* . . . 'Ordering! . . . One oysters, two foie gras . . . a scallop . . . followed by three sole . . . a lobster . . . one Chateau and a *poussin*!' crowed our chef. *Clack clack clack* . . . *dit dit dit*. The sound of paper being torn off. 'Two more oysters . . . two more foie . . . followed by three Dover sole! One lobster!' *Clack clack clack* . . . *dit dit dit* . . . and already I'm getting worried because they seemed to be hitting the sole hard. Each order took up a whole pan – a whole burner – meaning we could cook only four of the things at once. And sauté was also plating oysters because the lone salamander was on that station; so while I'd popped the hinges on three sheet pans of the things, the sauté guys still had to set them on rock salt, nape each oyster with sauce, brown them under the salamander, plate them, carefully top each one with an oh-so-delicate little heap of caviar (of which there was a limited amount), then garnish before putting them up in the window. The beggar's purses were inexplicably coming off that station too, with only the soup and the foie gras coming off Frankie's area.

The machine was printing full-bore now, paper spitting out end over end, and Bobby calling it all out and stuffing copies in the slide. So far we were keeping up, racing to drill out what we could before it really hit the fan.

Two big tables – a ten-top, and a twelve, one after the other – and still no main courses had been fired yet; I looked over and saw that sauté was already in the weeds, that Frankie was spazzing out on all the foie-gras orders, and that the truffle soup – which was supposed to be a layup – was not cooking as quickly as anticipated. Sure, the heating-the-soup part was a breeze, but the part where Frankie stretched precut squares of puff-pastry dough over the ovenproof crocks was taking a lot longer than hoped. Frankie was fumbling with the dough, which either broke because it was too cold from the refrigerator, or tore because it had been out of the refrigerator too long, or tore because Frankie was so high he was shaking – and Frankie wasn't so good at keeping a lot of orders in his head anyway, so the combination of minor frustration and all those foie gras and the fact that the little crustless pieces of brioche that were supposed to accompany it kept burning in the toaster was taking its toll, pulling down the pace . . . already the oysters were stacking up on one end, getting cold waiting for the foie-gras orders that were supposed to go with them, and Bobby (highest standards *only*, please) was sending them back for reheats and replates, which was causing some confusion as good became commingled with bad. And the printer kept clicking and the stack of orders that Bobby had yet to even call out while he waited for sauté and hot-app stations to catch up kept getting bigger and bigger (getting mixed up with the orders that he'd already called out and had yet to post in the slide), and it was clear, a half-hour in, with not a single main course served – or even fired – that we were headed for collision.

Bobby's reaction to the ensuing crisis was to urge on Frankie. Forcefully. Some might say, considering Frankie's known pathologies, too forcefully: 'Where's that FOIE, you idiot?! What the FUCK is up with that fucking FOIE!? What's WRONG with you, Frank? FRANK? Where's that fucking FOIE GRAS?'

Poor Frankie. He was spinning in place, trying to do ten things at once, and succeeding at none, eyes banging around in his skull, sweat pouring down his face, a dervish of confusion, the little four-burner stove full of melting foie gras and over-reducing sauce.

The runners' faces were starting to take on worried expressions as more time passed without anything coming up. A lone four-top went out – and was quickly returned as cold, causing Bobby to scream even more. Bobby tended to blame others in times of extremis. 'You *idiots*!' he'd yowl at the runners when yet another order of oysters was sent back, making our already-stressed-out runners even more jumpy. And the printer, all the while still clicking and clacking and going *dit dit dit* . . .

The first of the front waiters appeared, enquiring fearfully about app orders, which made Bobby even crazier. There were easily fifty tables' worth of orders up on the board, God knows how many in Bobby's hand, and a long white strip of them curling on to the floor that Bobby had yet to even acknowledge – and nothing was coming out of the kitchen. Nothing. Bobby finally managed to slap cloches on to a few orders of oysters and foie and send them on their way; and when he finally began to take stock of what he had in his hand, and what was still coming in, and how, by now, the sauté station had come to a complete standstill, I think his brain shut down. The next waiters who came in asking about food got shrieked at.

'Just GET OUT! GET OUT OF THE FUCKING KITCHEN!!'

The constant clicking from the computer, the background grumbling and swearing and cursing from the cooks, the back-and-forth questions necessary between line cooks working together like 'Ready on Table Seven? Ready on those oysters and that scallop?' and the occasional whispered request from a runner combined was too much noise for the chef. He shouted: 'SHUT UP! EVERYBODY SHUT THE FUCK UP! NOT A SINGLE FUCKING WORD! I WANT TOTAL SILENCE!'

He then issued orders for Matt to move some of the foie orders over to sauté, put Dougie in exclusive charge of the toaster, told Orlando and Steven both to get out of the way, and took over the sauté responsibilities himself, while abandoning expediting responsibility to me.

The pile of intermingled dupes I inherited was discouraging.

The board itself – meaning the orders that had already been begun, or fired – was a mess, with orders already dispatched mixed up with stuff still to come. I had no idea what had been called and what had yet to be called. Fortunately, the printer had calmed down. There was silence, *real* silence, as Bobby stepped into sauté and began putting together orders, running back and forth between hot-app station and his own to personally make sure tables were complete before putting them in the window.

We managed to get some apps out, and some more, and even a few more – before runners started whispering in my ear that they needed entrées, like *now*. The printer was strangely silent still, and I was thankful for it, figuring they were backed up at the terminals downstairs, or that maybe, just maybe, between all the orders in my hand and the ones that I was slowly feeding on to the board and the pile I was getting ready to call out, maybe we'd actually got the whole dining room in. I called out a few fire orders for mains but Bobby just screamed, 'SHUT UP! I DON'T WANT TO HEAR IT!' He was cooking foie-gras orders now, in addition to doing the oysters, and the beggar's purses, and dealing with the sole, and though a very fine line cook, he was biting off way more than he, or any cook alive, could chew. Alone in his head, out there on the edge all by himself, ignoring me, ignoring the waiters, ignoring the other cooks, he was slinging pans at high speed, just trying, as best he could, to knock down some of those hanging tickets, to get the food out. So I just kept my mouth closed and clutched my stack of dupes and held my breath.

The printer. Something was wrong with it. I knew it. It was too quiet. It had been too long. Not a click or a clack for twenty minutes, not a single fire code or dessert order. I checked the roll of paper. No jam. The machine seemed plugged in. Jumping on the intercom, I called Joe, the DJ and techie who knew about such things, and asked him discreetly to check and see if there was a problem.

Apparently there was. Suddenly the machine came alive, clacking away like nobody's business, spitting out orders in a terrifying, unending stream, one after the other after the other, faster than I could tear them off: twenty-five minutes of backed-up orders we hadn't even heard about. Worried front waiters entered the kitchen, took one look at what was going on, and retreated silently. Nothing to be done here.

It was clear to all of us by now – except maybe Bobby, who was still in his own ninth circle of personal restaurant hell, cursing and spitting and doing his best to cook, plate, and assemble orders, elbowing us out of the way as he ran heroically back and forth between stations – that we were now involved in a complete disaster. The situation was beyond saving. We could dig out . . . eventually. At some time, yes, we might feed these people. But we would not bring honour to our clan tonight. We would not go home proud. There would be no celebratory drinks at the end of this night (if it ever ended), only shame and recriminations.

Then I looked over at the kitchen doors and saw a particularly dismaying sight: three or four waiters clustered silently in the hallway. I hurried over to confer, away from Bobby's hearing. When waiters stop complaining, it is an unnatural thing. What were they doing out there? Things were bad in the dining room, I knew, but shouldn't they be down on the floor, putting out fires? Comping champagne? Reassuring their tables with self-deprecating apologies and offers of free cognac and port?

'What's up?' I enquired of the most reasonable of the lot, an aspiring playwright with many years of table-service experience.

'Dude . . . they're drunk out there,' he replied. 'They've been sitting out there without food for an hour and a half. Drinking champagne. They've got nothing in their bellies but alcohol – and they're getting belligerent.'

Veronica, a chubby waitress with (we had heard) a rose tattoo on her arse, was red-faced and shaking. 'A customer choked me,' she cried, eyes filling with tears. 'He stood up and put his hands around my neck and fucking *choked* me, screaming, "WHERE'S MY FUCKING FOOD?!" . . . It's out of control, Tony! I'm afraid to go out there. We all are!'

I rushed back to the kitchen, where Bobby was successfully putting out a few tables of appetisers. But orders were still coming back. There was more stuff coming back than going out, and with all the replates and refires, the caviar supply was running low.

'Bobby,' I said carefully. 'I think we should 86 the oysters.'

'We are *not* 86ing the fucking oysters,' snarled Bobby.

The kitchen doors swung open. It was Larry the waiter with tears running down his face. Now this was about as bad a sign as you could see, as Larry only moonlighted as a waiter. His day job was as a cop in the South Bronx. What, on the floor of a restaurant, could be so bad, so frightful, so monstrous as to cause a ten-year veteran of the force, a guy who'd been shot twice in the line of duty, to become so traumatised?

'They're beating the customers,' Larry wailed. 'People are getting up and trying to leave – and security is beating them! They're going fucking nuts!'

'It's out of control,' moaned Ed, the runner. 'It's a nightmare.'

NiteKlub, it should be pointed out, usually operated as

exactly that once the dinner shift was over. Consequently, we employed a security staff of twenty-three heavily muscled gorillas. These folks, though quite nice when not frog-marching you out the front door or dragging you down the steps, were employed to deal with the more rigorous demands of keeping order in a busy dance club: organised posses of gate-crashers, out-of-control drunks, belligerent ex-boyfriends – many of them potentially armed. They were frequently injured, often for giving a momentary benefit of doubt, for instance, to some barely-out-of-adolescence knucklehead half their weight denied entry to the VIP area, who promptly sucker-punched them or cold-cocked them with a beer bottle. This kind of thing gave our average security guy a rather shorter fuse than most ordinary restaurant floor staff. That this was a tonier crowd was a distinction security could hardly be expected to make. Especially as the customers were drunk and outraged at having spent hundreds of dollars for nothing, and heading for the doors in droves. Though they were said to be dealing out beat-downs to middle-aged couples from the suburbs who'd only wanted a nice New Year's Eve and some swing music, they could hardly be blamed for following the same orders they had been given every other night.

'I'm not going back out there. For anything,' said Larry.

We tried. We did the best we could that awful night. To his credit, Bobby cooked as hard and as fast as he could until the very end, pretty much doing everything himself, unwilling or unable to trust anyone to help him out of the hole he'd put us all in. It was probably the wisest thing to do. Between my calling and his cooking, there was a nice, direct simplicity, less chance of confusion. We served – eventually – a lot of cold baked oysters (many without caviar) and undercooked foie gras, leathery Dover sole and overcooked lobster, lukewarm birds and roasted beef.

1991 slipped into 1992 without notice or mention in the kitchen. No one dared speak. The word 'happy' in relation to anything would not have occurred to any of us. At twelve-forty-five, in what was perhaps the perfect coda to the evening, a lone, bespectacled customer in a rumpled tuxedo entered the kitchen, wandered up to the sauté end (where Bobby was still doing his best to get out entrées), and, peering back at the stove, asked, in a disconcertingly bemused voice, 'Pardon me . . . but is that my appetiser order?'

He'd been waiting for it since eight-forty-five.

I thought he'd showed remarkable patience.

At the end of the night, as it turned out, management had to comp (meaning return money) for $7,500 worth of meals. A few overzealous security goons had (allegedly) incited a few of our guests to file lawsuits claiming varying degrees of violent assault. And the effect on the kitchen staff was palpable.

Dougie and Steven quit. Adam became a titanic discipline problem, his respect for his chef declining to the point that it would, much later, lead to fisticuffs. Morale sank to the point that cooks arrived high – rather than waiting until later. And I got the chef's job after Bobby, wisely, went elsewhere.

And I learnt. Nobody likes a 'learning experience' – translating as it does to 'a total ass-fucking' – but I learnt. When the next year's New Year's Eve event loomed, I planned. I planned that mother like Ike planned Normandy. My menu was circulated (to management, floor and every cook), discussed, tested, and re-tested. Each and every menu choice was an indestructible ocean-liner classic – preseared or half-cooked hours before the first guest arrived. There wasn't an oyster in sight, or on any of the many New Year's menus I've done since. Just slice and serve terrine of foie gras. Slap-and-serve salads. *My* truffle soup the next year (it had been a good idea, actually) sat prebowled and precovered in a hot bain, ready to toss in the oven. I spread dishes around evenly between stations, imagining always the worst-case scenario. As, of course, I'd lived through it. My tournedos were preseared and required only a pop in the oven, some reheated spuds, a quickly tossed medley of veg, and a ready-to-pour sauce. My lobsters took a swift pop under the salamander. I'd be proud of the fact that *my* New Year's went flawlessly, that *my* full dining room of customers went home happy and content, and that I, unlike the vastly-more-talented-but-less-organised Bobby, brought honour and profit to my masters.

But the fact is, I could have served the following year's menu with a line crew of chimps. The food was nowhere as good as it could have been. My food arrived fast. It arrived hot. It arrived at the same time as the other orders on the table. But it was no better (or worse) than what a bunch of overdressed drunks dumb enough to eat at our club expected. Having tasted total defeat the previous year, when my last entrée went out at eleven-thirty, leaving only the mopping-up operations (aka desserts), I was ebullient. Not a single order had come back. I jumped up on the stainless-steel table we'd used to stack assembled dishes and beat my chest and congratulated one and all. We turned up the music, peeled off our reeking whites, changed into our street clothes, and I ordered us up a few pitchers of Long Island Iced Teas and beer. We drank like champions. And felt like champions. We went home exhausted but proud.

Sometimes, you just have to make compromises to get the job done.

What do you eat for breakfast?
Under ordinary circumstances – meaning when in New York – breakfast follows an invariable and health-friendly pattern: first – a cigarette. That first smoke of the day is also the best. Butt in hand, I'll toddle to the corner for a *New York Times* and two tall cups of coffee with cream and sugar. Then I'll sit in front of the computer, reading the paper, answering emails and smoking many more cigarettes – in between swigs of coffee. It strikes me as a healthy alternative to the more fattening breakfast options – and has the added attraction of leaving more room for a big lunch.

What dish would you cook in order to seduce someone?
Most would-be chef Lotharios cynically return to the classics when trying to dazzle a prospective bedmate: caviar, maybe some home-made blinis, perhaps a light yet technique-loaded menu (nothing too bloating) accompanied by champagne and yet more champagne. My thought is that the best thing to do is make the woman breakfast. At this point – presumably – you've already had your way with her. You've 'got what you wanted' – and the preparing of something as simple (yet impressive to watch) as an omelette and some freshly squeezed juice should strike your guest as an act of extraordinary selflessness and sensitivity.

What do you never cook?
I would never presume to cook traditional Chinese or Vietnamese food. They've been doing it for 6,000 years – it would seem presumptuous and somehow disrespectful (not to mention arrogant) to assume I had anything to add to the equation. And

you'll never catch me touching tofu or soya milk in any form in my kitchen.

What's the one dish you find hard to get right?
Baked goods hate me. They know I'm afraid, they sense my tenuousness and invariably fail me. On the rare occasions when I do cook at home, I buy out – or keep it very simple – like *crème renversée* or macerated fruit.

Two Great Tastes
that Taste Great Together

MICHELLE BERNSTEIN

A former dancer, Miami-born Michelle Bernstein is executive chef of 'MB' at the Aqua hotel in Cancún, Mexico. After graduating from Johnson & Wales University, Bernstein began her culinary career at Red Fish Grill and Christy's in Coral Gables, and Tantra in Miami Beach. She trained with Jean-Louis Palladin, and honed her skills at Alison on Dominick Street and Le Bernardin in New York. She then became executive chef and co-owner of the Strand, before drawing national attention as executive chef at Azul at the Mandarin Oriental hotel in Miami. For two years, she co-hosted the US Food Network's Melting Pot. Her new restaurant, Michy's, opened in Miami in 2006.

M Y FIRST KITCHEN job was as a line cook (*commis* in the industry vernacular), at Mark's Place in North Miami Beach, Florida. One night in 1993, during my second year on the job, we were expecting two celebrity guests. The one more familiar to our customers was TV's Maude, a famous *Golden Girl* in a town of real-life Golden Girls, the actress Bea Arthur. But the guest that sent shivers through the kitchen was the late great Jean-Louis Palladin, one of the few two- or three-Michelin-starred chefs ever to have opened a restaurant in the United States: Jean-Louis at the Watergate in Washington, DC.

Palladin was a legendary character in the industry. Though only in his late forties, he already possessed a famously craggy face, the product of equal parts hard work and hard living, and he had the wildly unkempt hair of a mad scientist. His temper reportedly knew no equal, but he was also appreciated for his genius, was considered a true friend to his peers, and was said to have a keen eye for recognising and appreciating talent and hard work.

Miami didn't have the number of great chefs and restaurants it does today, so this was a case of visiting royalty. Among our crew, I was the one most atwitter at the prospect of cooking for Chef Palladin, because our chef/owner Mark Millitello had arranged for me to leave my hometown of Miami and go and work for Palladin in Washington in just a few months.

My role in Mark's kitchen was an unusual one. I was far from the most seasoned cook, but I was a serial perfectionist. That, combined with the fact that I was the only woman in the house, made me – I guess – a nurturing presence, as much for my fellow cooks as for Mark. On days like this one, when something special was afoot, it was typical for Mark to tell people to 'run it by Michelle' before it left the kitchen.

Mark himself was a near nervous wreck about the visit; he spent the day in a tizzy, tasting and retasting every kitchen preparation, pulling out all the stops by embellishing the menu with extra touches. He and Jean-Louis had a passing acquaintance, as most US chefs of any renown do, but they weren't intimates, and any time a chef visited from another region, you wanted to make a good impression because other chefs were sure to get a report on the meal.

The most special thing Mark did to welcome Chef Palladin was to make a foie-gras terrine, one of the true labours of love in classic French gastronomy. Terrines require a deft hand and precise control throughout preparation, including careful monitoring of the temperature of the ingredients, both when you begin and when you stop cooking them.

I still remember the terrine that Mark made – featuring layers of foie gras and Sauternes gelée, made from the sweet dessert wine traditionally served alongside foie gras – a truly exemplary piece of craftsmanship that beautifully filled out its huge, rectangular, stainless-steel mould.

Because of my special role in that kitchen, I was entrusted with the terrine. In order to ensure it would be as smooth as possible when the time came to slice and serve it, Mark left it out on a shelf above my station for a few hours before service.

My mission was so clear that Mark didn't have to say a word: don't screw up, especially not with my future mentor in the house.

The kitchen at Mark's Place was cramped, to say the least. There was a front kitchen and a back kitchen, separated by a wall, a most unusual configuration. I was in the back area where we made appetisers and some pastries. Accordingly, my station was crowded with both the *mise en place* for salads and starters, and a huge bowl of warm chocolate sauce for topping various desserts.

Because of the kitchen's organisation, and our enormous menu (there were more than twenty appetisers), being a cook there required quite a bit of multitasking. It wasn't unusual for me to be plating a dish with one hand and whisking a dressing with another.

The only problem is that, even though I'm an ex-ballerina, I'm also something of a klutz, prone to minor accidents, spills, and such.

When the time came to send the terrine to Palladin's table, I arranged the salad plates on which I would serve it on my work station. I was putting salad on the plates with my left hand, and reaching up for the terrine with my right.

I didn't have a very firm grip on the terrine mould, so instead of lifting it, I only succeeded in pulling it off the shelf. It eluded my slippery fingers and tumbled down past my widening eyes right into the bowl of chocolate sauce, where it bobbed for a moment, like a ship with a hull breach taking on water, and then proceeded to sink into the murky depths.

As I reached in after it, my colleagues rushed over to help me try to save it – a difficult task. Had the terrine come straight from the fridge, it would have been hard and cold, and easy to wipe off. But softened as it was, and warming even more thanks to the chocolate, it was beginning to leach out into the sauce. Tan globules were bubbling up to the surface, turning the chocolate into a mocha-coloured nightmare.

I gingerly retrieved the unmoulded terrine from the sauce and laid it out on my station. The other cooks and I stood over it in our chocolate-spattered whites, trying to decide how to save our patient. The first step was to halt the melting and preserve its shape, and we worked on it furiously, smoothing it over with spatulas, and our fingers.

I was panicked beyond words.

But I also couldn't help recalling, with amusement, those old television commercials for Reese's Peanut Butter Cups I used to watch as a kid. Two individuals, hurried for no apparent reason – one carrying chocolate and one peanut butter – turn a corner and slam into each other, sending the chocolate into the peanut butter. They gasp in alarm, but needlessly so, because when they taste the resulting combination they realise that they've done the junk-food equivalent of discovering penicillin: peanut butter and chocolate, 'two great tastes that taste great together'.

Snobs might turn their nose up at this observation, but make no mistake about it: foie gras is the gourmet equivalent of peanut butter; insanely rich, it's best complemented by sweet or tart elements. Just as peanut butter goes with jelly, foie gras gets on famously with any number of fruit chutneys or compotes, like the Sauternes gelée with which it was layered in the terrine.

Along these same lines, it turned out, as we licked our fingers, that foie gras and chocolate – just like the commercials said – were two great tastes that tasted great together. I'd be lying if I denied that we were moaning with pleasure as we licked the bittersweet chocolate and molten foie gras from our fingers, the rich concoction sticking to the roofs of our mouths like, well, like peanut butter.

Though we'd saved the terrine from total destruction, some of the chocolate had fused with the foie into a coating that could not be removed without serious risk of destroying the whole thing.

Making peace with the situation, I continued plating the terrine, racing to finish before Mark could see it. He was anxious enough that Jean-Louis was in the house; finding out about the dive the terrine had taken into the chocolate might have put him over the edge.

Finally, I sent out our new special starter: 'chocolate-painted foie gras' with a lovely *mâche* salad.

I was too nervous to look out of the kitchen to see how the terrine went over, but it must have been fine because Jean-Louis's plates came back clean, and Mark didn't charge through the swinging kitchen doors screaming my name.

I came away from this incident unscathed. In fact, I got three things out of it. The first was a nickname by which my old pals from that kitchen still address me: Reeses.

The second is that, years later, when I had become executive chef of Azul at the Mandarin Oriental hotel on Miami Beach, I called on this episode to fashion one of my signature dishes: Seared Foie Gras with Chocolate *Mole*, *mole* of course being the savoury Mexican chocolate sauce.

If Mark reads this story, it'll be the first he's ever heard of the chocolate-painted terrine incident . . . because I never quite worked up the courage to tell him. I did tell Jean-Louis, though, during one of the rare times that, while working for the great chef, I found myself sharing a quiet moment with him. This was the third thing I got from that night: when I arrived at the punch line, Jean-Louis exploded with his huge, throaty laugh – I honestly don't think I've ever heard anyone laugh harder or louder – a cherished memory that alone made the whole thing worthwhile.

What do you eat for breakfast?
If I am not on a mad rush out the door, I make soft scrambled

eggs with chillies and onions, and toast and bitter orange marmalade. If I am running (twenty-five days out of the month) I drink enough coffee to choke a cow.

What dish would you cook in order to seduce someone?
If it was my husband . . . I wouldn't cook much – I would serve him oysters, caviar and blinis in a sexy get-up. But if it wasn't my husband I would definitely make him braised short ribs and mashed potatoes. Men are usually so 'meat-and-potato-minded'.

What do you never cook?
I am embarrassed as a chef to say this but I just can't cook venison. I have cooked and eaten ants, guinea pig, pig's head, live eels . . . I just love Bambi too much . . . but to heck with Thumper!

What's the one dish you find hard to get right?
Perfect *chicharones* (crispy pork skin). I mean I can make them pretty well, but for some reason they just never ever come out as good as the Cubans make them in the markets here in Miami. It really makes me crazy.

The Last Straw
MARIO BATALI

*One of the most recognisable food personalities in New York
City, Mario Batali is the chef and co-owner of a handful of
restaurants that have redefined Italian dining for New Yorkers
over the past decade: Del Posto, Babbo, Lupa, Esca, Otto
Enoteca Pizzeria, and others. Before he became a chef, restaurateur, cookbook author and television personality, Batali grew
up in Seattle, went to secondary school in Spain, and then
cookery school in London.*

As AUTUMN FELL on London in 1984, I was a student at
the local outpost of Le Cordon Bleu cookery school. For
extra money, I was a barman three nights a week at a big
working-class watering hole (we sold pints mostly, with the
occasional gin and tonic, no ice) on a piece of private property in
the middle of an essentially unremarkable road in central
London.

I hadn't been there long when the owners decided to convert

the pub into something much more ambitious: a 'serious' restaurant that served trendy, contemporary food, quite a sea change from the burgers and chips that were the top-selling items among our regulars. They blew out the back door of the place and performed an exhaustive renovation, transforming it – in a very efficient four weeks – into a sprawling restaurant with a garden out the back.

To create and execute a menu for the new restaurant, the owners installed a young chef we'll call Richard Lewison. Propriety prevents me from sharing his real name, but trust me, you've heard of him. He's the creative force behind a number of sickeningly successful restaurants in England. But at the time he was a complete unknown, one of countless young cooks who had toiled anonymously in the shadow of a couple of Michelin-starred restaurants.

Richard fashioned a two-man kitchen in the new restaurant, and I was kept on as the second man, quite an upgrade from barman in just four weeks. The kitchen was an open one, in full view of the diners, with a little station that had pendant heat lamps suspended over it where finished dishes took a moment in the spotlight before being shuttled to the appropriate table.

Richard was an amazingly fit guy, with a sinewy build that brought to mind a young boxer. This impression was reinforced by his frequent macho demonstrations, like his morning ritual of hoisting a fifty-pound bag of spuds up over his shoulder and depositing it in another part of the kitchen. (I'm not being a smartarse when I say that I think that was the highlight of his day.) He was also a very creative and thoughtful cook. Sure, he was copying the greats he had worked with, but that's a necessary rite of passage for any chef. At the same time, he was busy developing his own style, and there was much that a

young pup like myself could learn from a guy who hailed from a
Michelin darling like Le Gavroche.

For example, I saw up close and personal one of the great
efficiencies of a classic French kitchen: the use of 'mother sauces'
to create any sauce required for service. All of Richard's sauces
could be fashioned by embellishing one of the two bases we
made every morning. One was a classic mother sauce, hollandaise, an emulsification of egg yolks and clarified butter. The
other wasn't, strictly speaking, a mother sauce, but we used it as
one, and that was a *beurre blanc* (literally translated as 'white
butter'), a reduction of vinegar and shallots, to which butter was
added.

I mention this because, as you're about to learn, Richard was
given to the sort of fits common in European kitchens at the
time: big public outbursts that involved chewing out his staff
like Lee Ermey's drill sergeant in *Full Metal Jacket*. He'd get
right into your face and let you have it, with all kinds of weather
spraying forth from his mouth. (He also had his human moments and graces, like when he used the term of endearment
chups, by which he sometimes addressed me.) So, if you're
wondering why I put up with it, it's because it was worth
whatever it took to try to hang on, keep pace with him, and soak
up as much knowledge as I could.

Or perhaps I should say, it was worth it, *up to a point*. And
this, my friends, is the story of the day on which that point
revealed itself.

Now, Richard liked his hollandaise whipped to an extreme
froth. So every morning, I'd come in, make the yolk base, whip
it for what felt like an eternity, then work in the butter. I don't
know what, if anything, happened to him before he showed up

for work on the evening in question, but he came in, took one look at the hollandaise, and started in on me. 'What the fuck is this? What the fuck is this? There's no air in this!' I found this particularly annoying because when Richard got his back up, a French accent seeped into his voice ('*What zee fuk iz sis?*'), although, as far as I knew, he had never been to France in his life.

He then proceeded, right there in the open kitchen, with all of our customers looking on, to crack thirty-six eggs into a bowl and begin remaking the hollandaise. 'This is how you make it, with the air, with the air!' he announced as he whipped the yolks, shouting and gesturing wildly so everyone in the restaurant could see and hear. When he had finished, he handed me the bowl with a satisfied grin. I glanced down at it. The hollandaise he had produced was more or less identical to the one I had made. I'll grant him that perhaps it was *a bit* airier, but it was, for all intents and purposes, the same. It was the kind of thing I was used to, however, so I shrugged it off and got back to work.

Ten minutes later came the chips, which, like the sauces, were to be made fresh daily. Richard already had it in for the chips because he considered them beneath him; they were on the menu only because the owners insisted we have a burger and chips available for longtime customers who weren't about to order any dishes that involved a hollandaise sauce. After looking at the chips, Richard decided that I had cheated, making them the day before and stashing them in the walk-in. I assured him that I hadn't. In fact, I invited him to walk across the kitchen where he could see the evidence of freshness for himself: the spent potato peel, still in the rubbish bin.

But Richard didn't want to hear this. He so didn't want to

hear it that he called me a name he had never called me before: *navvy*. To this day, I'm not sure what it means, but *I think* it's a derogatory term that the Brits use to disparage the Irish. It has something to do with someone involved in the navigation or driving of a boat, like a merchant marine – in other words, an unskilled, menial labourer, a lowlife. When he called me that, a hush fell over the restaurant staff, as though Richard had just slapped me with his gloves and I was supposed to challenge him to a duel or something.

I didn't do that, but I did let him know that I didn't appreciate his disparagement, and he went after me for my supposedly unacceptable backtalk. We never came to physical blows, but things got verbally violent. Then, as always, they subsided, and we forgot about it and got back to work.

Shortly thereafter, one of our more important customers, the owner of a nearby antiques shop, came in for dinner and ordered one of the evening's specials. Richard prepared the meat, then summoned me for my contribution: 'Mario, quick, bring me the sautéed courgette that goes with this.' I brought it over. A moment later, Richard stopped what he was doing: 'Chups, come and look at these, they're not right.'

I had no idea what he was talking about. In the pan were perfectly cut matchsticks of courgette, glistening in oil, cooked through but with just the right amount of bite left in them.

'But, Chef, this is how we've been doing the courgettes for the past two days.'

'This is not the way we do them! This will never be the way we do them! This is not Michelin-star food!'

But we're not a Michelin-star restaurant, I thought, though didn't dare say it.

Richard dumped the courgettes and I made him a fresh batch,

more or less identical to the first, but somehow acceptable this time.

A little while later, another gentleman joined the antiques-shop owner at his table and ordered risotto with calf's liver. That's when things really got cooking in the kitchen.

'Mario, bring over the risotto,' Richard said, summoning me again.

I obliged. Richard took one glance at the risotto and pro-claimed it undercooked.

'Richard,' I said, 'this is *al dente* risotto. This is how we serve it here.'

'Who's the chef here?'

'You're the chef here, Chef.'

I don't know if he thought I was being sarcastic, or if maybe he detected just a smidge of had-enough-of-your-shit in my voice, but that was it. He slapped the hand in which I was holding the pan and unloaded a mess of adjectives on me, the whole drill-sergeant bit again.

'Dude,' I said, 'this is perfect risotto.'

'Perfect? This is not perfect! You'll have to cook it again!'

'Aw, for the love of fuck . . .'

Here came the French accent again: '*For zee love of fuk? For zee love of fuk?*'

And with that, he picked up the offending pan of risotto and hurled it across the five-foot space that had grown between us during the argument. The pan hit me smack in the chest before tumbling down to the ground, spilling its contents all over the newly renovated floor.

There wasn't anything else to be said. I turned my back on Richard, walked into the prep area at the rear of the kitchen, and took a fistful of salt in one hand. I paused and looked over at Richard. He had his back to me and was finishing the dish without the risotto, putting on his little show for the customers. I tossed the salt into the *beurre blanc*. Took another fistful and tossed it in the hollandaise. Then I took off my apron, threw it in the linen bin, and – having satisfied my appetite for knowledge and revenge at this particular place of employment – walked out the back door and into the cool London night, a *navvy* no more, whatever the hell that meant.

What do you eat for breakfast?
I like leftover spicy Chinese or Thai, cold meatballs or pasta with hot sauce on it.

What dish would you cook in order to seduce someone?
Spaghetti with aubergine and chilli.

What do you never cook?
I never *never* cook.

What's the one dish you find hard to get right?
I'm a pro: this does not happen.

The Blind Line Cook
GABRIELLE HAMILTON

Gabrielle Hamilton is the chef-owner of Prune, which she opened in New York City's East Village in October 1999. Prune was named in Time Out New York's 2000 Top 100 *and Gael Greene's 'Where to Eat in the New Millennium' in* New York magazine, *and also featured in* Saveur 100 *in 2001. She has written for* The New Yorker, Saveur *magazine, and* Food & Wine *and had the eight-week Chef's Column in the* New York Times. *Her work has been anthologised in* Best Food Writing 2001, 2002, *and 2003.*

A COUPLE OF YEARS AGO I placed an ad for a line cook. And there was a guy who, according to his résumé, should have been right up my alley. He held a lunch-chef position in a busy seafood joint at the Jersey Shore; he had a bachelor's degree in political philosophy; and he had about six years of experience in the industry. I was looking forward to meeting this guy from my own home state, with whom an after-work conversation over beers might be possible, and who had just enough years in the industry still to have something to learn, but not so few that he would need to be taught everything. I called him up and we had a pleasant phone exchange. I liked his voice, his manner; he was intelligent and articulate. I invited him in for an interview the following day.

The first thing I noticed when he arrived was that he was blind. His eyes wandered around in their sockets like tropical fish in the aquarium of a cheap hotel lobby. We managed a handshake and sat at the bar. I asked him about his responsibilities as a lunch chef at the busy seafood restaurant and he answered entirely reasonably. He understood the language I used and spoke it back to me: the sort of shorthand code that people who work in kitchens speak.

I said, 'How many covers for lunch?'

And he said, 'Eighty-five to one ten.'

I said, 'What kind of *mise* is there in a fried seafood place?'

And he laughed and said, 'Yeah, it's all lemon wedges and tartare sauce.'

We talked a bit about his education in political philosophy: he was a Hegel fan. Finally, I showed him our menu. He held it up to his face as if to breathe in its written contents, to discover by inhaling what it said in plain print. I felt more certain than ever when I observed this that he was blind, but naturally doubted myself because obviously the guy had worked in restaurants, which – though we may joke – really can't and shouldn't be done. And in spite of the proximity of the menu to his face, I thought maybe I was making some despicable assumptions about the 'sight-impaired' and needed to get my politics up to date.

So I booked him for a trail.

I went downstairs and unpinned the schedule from the cork board and pencilled him into the grill station the next night. He wrote his new phone number on the top of his résumé in large unwieldy script and even managed, more or less, to locate and cross out the old number. I looked at him as directly in the eyes as one could, thinking maybe I should ask about what seemed obvious, but instead I said, 'Well, you seem average in build – we have pants and jackets in the general human range so you don't need to bring your own whites. And you'll just need a chef knife, a utility, and a paring knife. No need to bring your 40-pound kit tomorrow.' He nodded, without returning my gaze.

'Is there anything else you can think of?' I asked hopefully. He said only that he'd like to keep the menu if I didn't mind so he could study it a bit before his trail. Done deal. We shook hands again, miraculously.

For the rest of the day I thought maybe he wasn't blind, and that just because his eyes rolled around didn't mean he couldn't make out shape and colour. But then I thought *shape shmape* and *colour schmolour*, how is this guy going to dice a white onion on a white cutting board? I thought maybe I was an ignorant asshole who didn't realise how far the blind had come. Maybe he had worked out some kind of system to compensate. I took a mental inventory of famous accomplished blind people. Could playing the piano be anything like grilling fish over open flame, in the midst of hot fryer fat, sharp knives, macho line cooks, and slippery floors? What was the preferred term for blind these days, anyway? I wondered.

By the morning of his trail, I had talked myself into the certainty that, though blind, he was obviously 'sighted' in some other way. I felt sure that I was behind the times for thinking that, just because someone was blind, they couldn't work a job as a line cook in a busy restaurant. Or even be the lunch chef of one, as his résumé claimed. I knew, vaguely, that when a person lost one sense, the others kicked in expertly to compensate. I assured myself that he had developed a system by which he *heard* the food, or *felt* the food, or smelt which plate was used for which entrée. I became convinced that he, in fact, had evolved into such a higher species of line cook that we would learn greatness from him. I got so 'on board' with the whole blind-line-cook thing that I was plainly righteous when asked by my incredulous – and slightly unnerved – line cooks why I had booked a trail with a blind guy. I practically had indignation in my tone. 'What? You think just because the guy is *visually challenged* that he can't cook in a restaurant?'

When he arrived, I took him around on an introductory tour of the prep area and the walk-in and the hot line. At each station, he bent over and put his forehead against everything I showed him. It was fascinating at first – and later, heartbreaking – to note the angle at which he scrutinised each item in the refrigerator.

'Over here,' I said, 'is where all the proteins are kept. Fish here. Meat here. Cooked above raw. Always. OK?' And instead of holding the six-pan of pork belly close under his nose and squinting down upon it – like a very old man might do trying to read his train ticket – he instead held each item up to his forehead, above his eyebrows, and stared up imploringly into it.

We set him up in the basement prep area with a cutting board and a menial task that wouldn't matter if he screwed it up: picking parsley. This took him most of the afternoon and it was painful to watch him bent in half, killing his back in order to have his untethered eyes close to the cutting board.

The trail is simply the time to sniff out the guy, to see how he stands, how he holds his knives, how much he talks or doesn't, and what he says. Does he ravage everything with tongs or finesse with a fork and a spoon? Does he sit at the bar at the end of his trail and get hammered? Did he bring a pen and small pad of paper? Did he thank the people who trailed him? I wasn't worried that he was supposed to hold down the grill station. And I didn't give a shit about the parsley. But I understood twenty-five minutes into his trail that there was no system of compensation, he had not become hypersensate, and that he had not, emphatically, evolved into a superior cooking machine. Sadly, the guy was just plain blind. And I still had on my hands another four hours and thirty-five minutes of a trail to honour.

The night started slowly with just a couple of tickets at a time. I buckled myself into a seat at the back of the bus, so to speak, right behind the blind guy in the grill station, and let my sous-chef do the driving: calling out the tickets and their timing, expediting their plating and pickups. Every time an order came into our station, I quietly narrated the procedure to the trailer, and watched, slack-jawed, as he painstakingly retrieved a portion of meat from the cooler, held it to his forehead, set it on a plate, and then proceeded carefully to season the countertop with an even sprinkling of salt. When the call to 'fire' an item came, I stood back and let him place the meat on to the grill – which he managed – but I had to pull him back a few inches from the flames so he wouldn't singe his hair.

Eventually we fell into a kind of spontaneous, unfunny vaudeville routine in which I shadowed him, without him knowing, and seasoned the meat he missed, turned the fish he couldn't, moved the plate under his approaching spatula to receive the pork, like an outfielder judging a flyball in Candlestick Park. I was not worried about him slowing down the line as we never expect a trailer actually to perform a vital function. But I really started to feel sick with worry when he pulled a full, fresh, piping-hot basket of shoestring fries up out of the fat with his right hand and turned them out to drain – not into the waiting stack of giant coffee filters he held in his left hand, but into the thin air directly adjacent, pouring them out on to the dirty rubber mats and his clogs.

This did not escape the notice of the other cooks. All the lightheartedness of a good night on the line went right up the exhaust hood. The banter between *garde manger* and sauté came to a screeching halt. The fun part of getting through the night – donkey noises, addressing the male line cooks as 'ladies', as in 'Let's go, ladies!' – was abandoned. The stern but soft-hearted barking from the bus driver down the line lost all playful bite and got tamed down to the most perfunctory, gently articulated, 'Please fire apps on seven.' With one basket of hot fries cascading to the ground we all saw at once that this fellow was in physical danger.

In silence, I raked the fries up from the floor, trashed them, and dropped another order on the double. I asked him, kindly, to step back to the wall and just watch a bit, explaining that the pace was about to pick up and I wanted to keep the line moving. This is – even when you have all your wits – the most humiliating part of a trail: when the chef takes you off the line in the middle of your task. You die 1,000 deaths. For a blind guy with something to prove, maybe 2,000.

To this point I had been somehow willing to participate in whatever strange exercise this guy was putting himself through. I was suspending disbelief, like we're asked to do every time we go to see a play or watch a movie. *I know that this isn't real but I agree to believe that it is for these two hours without intermis-*

sion. But something about the realisation of the danger he was flirting with in service of his project, whatever his project was, suddenly pissed me off. I took over the station and started slamming food on to the plates, narrating my actions to him in barely suppressed snide tones. 'This,' I practically hissed, 'is the pickup on the prawns. Three in a stack, napped with anchovy butter. Wanna *write that down*?'

I exhausted myself with passive-aggressive vitriol. 'On the rack of lamb, you want an internal temp of one twenty-five. Just *read the thermometer*, OK.'

This got the attention of my sous-chef, who quietly came over and asked the guy if he'd like to step into *garde manger* for a while to see how things there ran. I was relieved to have the guy away from the fire and the fat and in the relatively harmless oasis of cold leafy salads and cool creamy dressings. And I was grateful to be rescued from my worst self. The guy spent the rest of his trail with his back up against the wall in all the stations, eyes rolling around in his head, pretending to apprehend how each station worked. I spent the remainder of his trail wrestling meat and unattractive feelings triggered by this insane predicament in which we had found ourselves.

I have never known what he was doing. I allowed him to finish out the whole trail, and when he had changed his clothes, I encouraged him to sit at the bar and have something to eat, which he did. And as he was leaving I said I would call him the next day, which I did. I told him that I was looking for someone with a little more power, a bit more of a heavy-hitter, but that I would keep him in mind if a position more aligned with his skills became available. This, remarkably, he seemed to see coming.

What do you eat for breakfast?

I have coffee with half and half and whatever disgusting bites of mashed crap my one-year-old son insists on feeding me while I try to feed him. (He already has the inclination to feed others.) We usually have several spoons going at once with yoghurt and cereal and banana, so that at some point at least one of them makes it into his maw, but there have been plenty of breakfasts of goldfish and popcorn, I won't lie.

What dish would you cook in order to seduce someone?

If I wanted to seduce someone, I would take them to IKEA, skip the showroom full of flimsy press-board furniture and head right to the cafeteria where I would buy them a cold shrimp-salad open-faced sandwich with hard-boiled egg and mayonnaise on rye bread as an appetiser and then the ten-piece Swedish meatball plate with gravy, dilled Red Bliss potatoes, and lingonberry sauce. Equally, I would marry the person who thought to do the same for me.

What do you never cook?

I never cook fruit with meat or otherwise pair sweet things with savoury things like foie gras with all those cloying fruit compotes, or pork with apples, or duck with figs, or chicken with raisins. I always want more of the salty or acidic or bitter aspect of the main component.

What's the one dish you find hard to get right?

It's not a particular dish I find hard to get right, but rather it's the dish I persist in finishing even though I know I have missed out a component or step of it along the way. Sometimes I just want a break, in spite of my short cut or haste or negligence, and I want the dish to turn out even though I know perfectly well in my heart that it won't because of whatever error I pretended wasn't significant. Does that make sense? It's like wanting to cheat and not get caught.

A User's Guide to
Opening a Hamptons Restaurant

PINO LUONGO

Born in of Tuscany, Pino Luongo is the unstoppable force behind some of New York City's most influential Italian restaurants, including the groundbreaking Il Cantinori, which he opened in 1983. Other Luongo classics include Coco Pazzo and Centolire. The author of four cookbooks, Luongo was also the subject of a memorable chapter in Anthony Bourdain's Kitchen Confidential. *Some of Luongo's restaurants, like Sapore di Mare, Mad 61, and Le Madri, have faded into history, but still conjure fond memories for those who dined there.*

I GREW UP IN Tuscany, and some of my happiest recollections are of summers at the beach in Porto Ecole and Porto Santo Stefano, where the sun shone brightly all day and my friends and I spent months splashing in the surf, cruising around in our convertibles, and eating by the shore. Music from those long-ago days still echoes in my mind, like Mungo Jerry's 'In the Summertime' or those opening piano blasts of the Beatles' 'The Long and Winding Road', taking me right back to 1971.

I came to New York City in 1980, and three years later, I opened my first restaurant, Il Cantinori, a menuless trattoria on East Tenth Street where we served different dishes every night based on the market and my mood. It was a sensation and, though I haven't been a part of it for a long time, still does a solid business.

As much as I loved living in New York City (and still do), I had come to miss the ocean. Manhattan is surrounded by water, of course, but we're talking rivers – sluggish, filthy rivers that separate it from New Jersey and the outer boroughs. So in the fall of 1986, I decided to spend some time by the beach, in the fabled Hamptons.

If you don't know, the Hamptons are a weekend playground for the rich and famous, about two hours east of the city, or four hours on a summer Friday when the Long Island Expressway is jammed beyond belief.

The Hamptons are where everyone from Puff Daddy to Steven Spielberg go to relax, be seen, and luxuriate in their palatial homes. They have been fashionable for ever: *The Great Gatsby* takes place in the Hamptons, even though F. Scott Fitzgerald made up different names for them.

I never cared one way or another about the scene out there. What I loved was being near the ocean. It just makes me feel good – so good that I didn't even care if it was summer or not; the first time I rented in the Hamptons was in the off season, from Labor Day through Memorial Day, instead of the other way around.

I was newly married and my wife, Jessie, and I took a house

that wasn't winterised. It was chilly and draughty and the toilet water froze, but it was near the Napeague Bay, not far from Montauk, so I was happy to be there.

I remember driving around the Hamptons in those dark, winter days and thinking to myself how few restaurants there were in the towns along 27, the Montauk Highway, which connects the dots on the Hamptons map, from Southampton to Bridgehampton to East Hampton and on out to Montauk.

There's so little action, I thought. In the summer this place must be magic.

Inspired by the proximity to water and by a fierce longing for summer, I began to envision a restaurant that would capture all the charm of Porto Ecole and Porto Santo Stefano, a restaurant that could re-create those long-ago days – that sense of summer, salt, sand, tanned skin, and the simple food that brought each day to a perfect close.

I started tapping the steering wheel, singing 'In the summertime, when the sun goes down . . .'

Later that winter, I was driving along 27, about to round the bend into East Hampton, when I passed what looked like a haunted house. Formerly the home of Charlotte's the Hidden Pond restaurant, and before that the home of a state senator, the property was available and the owners had gone into bankruptcy, explained a sign.

The place was an eyesore: a Tudor-style English house with a dark wooden frame and a sad grey tint to the stucco. It was in merciless disrepair, with huge nicks in the walls and cracks in the wood.

But I saw potential in it, and I loved that it was situated at the end of one of the splits of Georgica Pond, which flows alongside 27 where Bridgehampton and East Hampton meet. Plus, I fancy myself the Bob Vila of the restaurant industry, able to turn 'this old restaurant' into something shiny and new.

So it was that, in February 1987, I assumed ownership of the space and went to work transforming it into a spot-on replica of a Mediterranean villa, with tile floors, terracotta accents, and lots of wide-open spaces through which the summer breeze could blow, carrying that precious scent of the sea right through the dining room.

I named my new pet project Sapore di Mare, meaning 'taste of the sea', and we opened on 23 May 1987. The restaurant exceeded my wildest hopes: it was an instant success. Friends and customers from the city, many of whom had weekend homes in the Hamptons, showed up in our first days and weeks, and their reaction was a unanimous, 'Wow.'

But I'll tell you something: I was banging out the wrong song on my steering wheel the fateful day that I spotted this space. I should've picked 'The Long and Winding Road', because that's what it was like operating a restaurant out there. Really long, and really fucking winding.

We had a good run at Sapore di Mare, but we also had our challenges. And many of them were challenges unique to this kind of moneyed, resort community. So, for anyone out there interested in opening a restaurant in the Hamptons, here's my hard-earned advice:

1. Don't Hire Your Own Family

A constant struggle in the early days of Sapore di Mare was that the Hamptons' supply of seasoned hospitality professionals was very poor.

I was blessed with a great chef, an American named Mark

Strausman who cooks with the soul of an Italian and later became my chef at Coco Pazzo; and a maître d' named Ariel Lacayo, a sharply dressed, smooth-tongued Latin American who works with me today at Centolire, where people still remember him from those days at the beach.

But we had big problems finding support in the kitchen or the dining room. It quickly became apparent that, no matter how many ads we ran in the paper, and no matter how many phone calls I made, we were going to have trouble filling all the positions. As for the few employees that we *did* manage to find – locals who had worked in diners and greasy-spoon joints – they could barely handle the pressure. Most of them stopped showing up for work after a few days, never to be heard from again.

I was able both to cook and work the dining room, but you can only do so much at once. So, when we opened, I told Ariel to keep the crowd to a manageable size, even turning away business if necessary. And to make sure that he didn't cave into the pressure of clamouring customers, I asked Jessie, then five months pregnant, to work the door with him.

This was a sound enough plan, but the Hamptons in the summer are populated with everyone who ever set foot in Il Cantinori, or so it seemed. So, as the hour approached eight o'clock each evening, the phone began to ring. Jessie would dutifully tell all comers that we were fully booked. In most towns, that would have been the end of the discussion.

But not in the Hamptons.

In fact, there was no *discussion*. A typical exchange went like this:

Ring. Ring.

JESSIE: Hello?

CUSTOMER: This is Ms So-and-So. Do you have a table available at 9 p.m.?

JESSIE: No, I'm sorry, we're fully booked.

CUSTOMER: Just tell Pino we're coming over.

JESSIE: But . . .

Click. Dial tone. Sound of Jessie slamming down the phone.

'Tell Pino we're coming over,' was the most-uttered phrase in the Hamptons that summer, along with 'I'm a friend of Pino's,' favoured by guests who didn't even bother to call, and instead just showed up, their version of 'Open Sesame.'

About once a night, poor Jessie would come swinging through the door to the kitchen, which opened right on to the pasta station, where I usually cooked. She would tell me of the latest inhuman treatment she had received, and then sulk back to the dining room.

It breaks a man's heart to see his wife look so sad, especially when she's trying to help him out. But what could I do? I needed somebody I could trust minding the store.

And so it went in those early days, the rousing success marred only by my wife's misery.

One night, I was going about my business at the pasta station when I had that sixth-sense intuition, unique to chefs and restaurateurs, that I had better go check on the dining room. I did: everything was fine. But my radar wasn't totally busted. Sitting *on* the reservation desk was Jessie, staring off into space, shell-shocked.

It was clear that this couldn't continue. All that lay ahead for me was trouble: a series of tense battles on the home front, the evil product of seeds planted in the restaurant. Moments later, as I watched my dear wife withstand an earful of abuse from yet another unannounced group, I decided that I had no choice. I had to get rid of her.

But I couldn't bring myself to fire her.

At the end of the night, I pulled Ariel aside and told him, 'Tomorrow morning, the moment you get up, find me a new hostess. Don't go to the beach. Don't come in here. Get on the phone and find me someone and have her here by three-thirty,' an hour before Jessie's scheduled arrival.

The next day, Ariel had a new hostess installed, as directed. When Jessie showed up, she jerked a thumb in the girl's direction and asked Ariel what was going on.

'Pino had to replace you,' he said, trying to sound soothing on my behalf. 'It was too much stress for you.'

'Oh really?'

Jessie came swinging into the kitchen and stared at me with a look so cold that the pasta water stopped boiling. 'You know, I really don't care about working here,' she screamed. 'I was trying to help you out. But you . . . you . . . you coward. You couldn't tell me yourself?'

'That's right,' I said. 'I couldn't do it. But what's important is I'd rather keep you as a wife than as an employee.'

I guess I was losing my touch as a ladies' man, because she spun round in a rage and stomped out of the kitchen. But she was home that night when I got back from work, and though she didn't admit it right away, she was happier. We have three kids today and a good marriage, and it's all because I did the right thing and replaced her that night, sparing her any more indignities at the hands of my dear Hamptons customers.

2. Don't Hire Your Customers' Family

That first summer, while I was in New York City running Il Cantinori during the week, I would get frantic calls from Mark, the chef, increasingly concerned by our lack of help. Our employment problems continued unabated and we were only getting busier and busier. If I had known what an ongoing headache this would be, I probably never would have opened the restaurant.

I was in a desperate situation, so when two of my regular customers (too ridiculously affluent and influential to name) asked me to give their home-from-college kids – we'll call them Mitch and Missy – summer jobs, I thought, Sure, why not? And I hired them as a busboy and busgirl.

Before we go any further, you have to understand that I come from an Italian family and that we pride ourselves on our work ethic. The idea that some people simply have no pride whatsoever was completely beyond me.

But I got a quick lesson.

The trouble started almost immediately, when Missy showed up for her first day at work in her BMW convertible and parked it in the lot next to the highway. Our innkeeper, a very serious old Dominican, instructed her to park it out back – the front lot was for customers. 'Oh, Chico,' she said to him without breaking stride, her blonde hair flowing behind her in the summer wind, 'I *am* a customer.'

Instead of showing up at five minutes to four, like the employees who needed the job, she and Mitch showed up at four-thirty, fresh from the beach, unkempt, and smelling of the sea and sand.

'You, boy,' I said to the young man. 'Do you have a watch?'

'Yes, Mr Luongo.'

'What time are you supposed to be here?'

'Four o'clock.'

'And what time is it?'

He looked down at his Rolex. 'Four-thirty.'

'So?'

'I'm sorry, Mr Luongo. I fell asleep at the beach.'

I looked at his unshaven face, his salt-caked hair. 'What are you going to do about a shower?'

'Oh, I don't need a shower, Mr Luongo. I'm just a busboy.'

'Just a busboy? Look at these other people who are "just busboys",' I said, gesturing at the well-groomed crew, in freshly cleaned black slacks and white shirts: my proud, hard-working team.

'How many times have you come to my restaurant? Do the busboys look like this?' I pointed at him, to make sure he understood what *this* meant.

'You're right, Mr Luongo. I'm sorry. It'll never happen again.'

Once they got to work, things weren't much better. Missy had an aversion to soiled dishes, an unfortunate trait in a busgirl. When she approached an abandoned table, with its half-eaten pastas, napkins dropped in sauce and cigarette butts in the wine glasses, she would scrunch up her face and hold her breath. Then, to avoid breaking a nail, she would only pick up one or two dishes at a time, scurry to the kitchen with them, and come back for the next puny load.

On a scale of one to ten, I'd say she was a minus ten.

As if I didn't have enough problems to deal with, every time I left the kitchen, I'd find these kids doing something unbelievable. Like the time I discovered them in the middle of Saturday-night service, passing a cigarette back and forth in the parking lot out behind the kitchen. Or when they took a break that same night to sit at the bar and have a cocktail.

When I saw *that*, I pulled them aside.

'Kids, listen. In Italy, we have an expression that if you look the other way three times, you are stupid. And I'm starting to feel like an idiot.'

I presented them with a choice: 'I'll give you one more chance. Be here at four o'clock tomorrow. *Or else.*'

Mitch – he's probably a lawyer today – jumped right in. 'Yes, Mr Luongo. That's perfect. I feel like the past few day we've just been breaking the ice.'

'Listen,' I said. 'We're not breaking the ice. You're breaking my balls. Now get out of here.'

The next day, with a fool's optimism, I pushed myself all morning and into the afternoon. I got *my* work done early so I could spend some time with Mitch and Missy when they arrived, show them how I expected them to work, turn them into the kind of proud workers I respected.

I had been a busboy in my life. I had done everything you could do in a restaurant, and that's part of why I resented them so much. I didn't care who their parents were; the fact that they thought they could disrespect my beautiful Sapore di Mare, the place I had built with my own sweat and hard work – that was the most offensive thing of all.

You already know what happened next. They didn't show up at four o'clock. They didn't even show up by four-fifteen. When they finally did show up, at four-thirty, I was sitting in the balcony overlooking the dining room. I watched them prance in through the front door, even though Chico – hard-working,

proud Chico – told them not to every day. As always, they were
fresh from the beach, with messy hair and that salty smell.

I don't know how much you know about the restaurant
industry in New York, but if you read the papers here in the
1980s, then you might have heard I had a temper in those days.
I'm not going to deny it. I had a massive temper. And this was
the kind of thing that set it off.

'You two,' I said as I stood up and charged down the stairs.
They looked terrified, like they were about to be gored by a bull.

'You know what? That's it. You better get out of here. In fact,
you better get out of here right now. Actually, you know what,
GET THE FUCK OUT OF HERE. NOW!'

They didn't move.

'NOW!'

'But, Mr Luongo,' Mitch said. 'What about our tips from last
night?'

'*Tips?*' I actually laughed. 'You want your tips? I'll give you a tip:
you go home and tell your fathers that you are *fired*. You incom-
petent, spoilt, rich brats.' They stood there for a second, in shock.

Mitch jerked his head in the direction of the bar, suggesting to
Missy that they have a drink before leaving.

'Now!' I bellowed. 'Get the fuck out of here, you little brats.
Out, out, out,' and I chased them right out the door.

Both Mitch's and Missy's fathers called me, outraged, vowing
that they'd never come back to Sapore di Mare again.

But they did. They had to. They were friends of Pino's.

3. Teach Your Employees English

It's pretty common to have restaurant employees who don't
speak English. It's so common that there's a pamphlet-sized

book sold in certain industry-supply shops called *Kitchen Spanish*. But if you ever open a restaurant in the Hamptons, teach your employees English. Or you might find yourself without a staff.

One summer day when I was working in the city as usual, Mark called me from Sapore and told me the following story:

It was a quiet weekday, and in the Hamptons, it gets so quiet that you can stand along the highway and hear the wind blow through the trees. All of a sudden, out of nowhere, five black sedans screeched into the Sapore di Mare parking lot and surrounded the building.

A group of federal agents marched into the place and began interrogating everybody on the staff. They didn't check for proof of citizenship or ask to see green cards. Any employees who didn't speak English were simply corralled and taken away in the cars, off to who-knows-where.

'Thank God I can still manage a Brooklyn accent or they might have taken *me*,' Mark said.

I hung up the phone and looked around the kitchen. My crew was finishing their prep for that night's dinner. The *mise en place* containers – the little stainless-steel vessels in which prepared ingredients are held along the line – were full and, having been there since the early morning, the crew was winding down and thinking about going home for the day.

'Guys, listen up.' I told them what had happened at Sapore, and that I needed them to go out to my car. I was going to drive them to the Hamptons, they would work a shift out there, and I'd have them back by morning.

'Pino, no, please no,' they begged.

But I had no choice. We had to be ready for dinner at the beach. So we piled into the car, drove out to the Hamptons, and

I assigned each of them to a station. They were real troupers, prepping and then cooking all night, only to pile back into my car at eleven-forty-five that night for the return trip to Manhattan.

The next day, I got my Sapore staff back. They weren't happy, and neither was I. I suppose I could've sued the government, but I had other priorities, like replenishing my ever-dwindling reservoir of employees, a task that had become even harder that morning with the new prerequisite that they speak English.

4. All Rules Are Open to Interpretation

One of my favourite images from Sapore di Mare was Ralph Lauren.

Not the brand. The man.

Within a few months of Sapore's opening, the clientele began taking the summertime theme to extremes. They'd show up looking as though they had just come from the beach, which I'm sure many of them had. There were wearing shorts, sandals, even bathing suits.

Many of our customers understood the spirit of Sapore, and would arrive in casual but elegant attire. The bathing-suiters, however, were rapidly becoming the majority.

So we made a new rule: no shorts. Just like at the Vatican.

And then one night Ralph Lauren, driving home with his wife and a few friends, decided to drop in for dinner. The friends met our dress code, but Ralph was wearing shorts.

Ralph Lauren in shorts doesn't look like most people in shorts. I didn't see him when he came in, but I'm sure he was as fashionable as ever.

Nonetheless, Ariel didn't want to make any exceptions. We didn't keep any pants in the cloakroom the way some restaurants keep jackets. So my quick-thinking maître d' ran into the kitchen and emerged with a pair of black-and-white checked chef pants, presenting them to Ralph Lauren.

Ralph, gentleman that he is, disappeared good-naturedly into the men's room and emerged in his new outfit.

By the time I heard what had happened and caught up with Ralph, I was mortified. But Ralph is a sport. He said it was no big deal and that he was happy to comply.

And, you know what? He looked good. He looked so good that I'm surprised chef pants didn't become the next big fashion craze out there.

Even in the Hamptons, I guess, absurdity has its limitations.

5. Most Mistakes Can Be Corrected

OK, after all this bad news, let me share a story with a happy ending.

Saturday afternoon at Sapore was the eye of the storm between Friday night and Saturday night. It was also a time when many of our celebrity customers came in for lunch, to enjoy the restaurant's patio away from the eyes of the masses.

One Saturday afternoon, we were hosting Billy Joel and Christie Brinkley, along with their little daughter Alexis, and another couple who have also since gone their separate ways, Alec Baldwin and Kim Basinger.

I was busy in the kitchen, getting ready for the evening service. The only management presence in the dining room was the current occupant of our revolving-door position of receptionist-hostess.

At about three o'clock, I began thinking about the dinner hour and went into the dining room to see if Ariel had shown up yet. There he was, the picture of Hamptons style, in a white linen suit with brown-leather slip-on shoes.

With a list of that night's reservations in hand, we walked the floor together, determining who we'd seat where, a very political exercise at a hot spot like Sapore. We also personally greeted Alec and Kim and Billy and Christie, all of whom were regulars, and – I must say – absolutely charming.

As we made the rounds I noticed, out of the corner of my eye, pedalling up to the entrance on a bicycle, a woman in her mid-sixties, or so I'd have guessed. It was tough to tell: she was wearing a straw hat and sunglasses so it was hard to see her face.

But something about her seemed familiar.

We couldn't hear the exchange that followed, but from the gestures – the woman spoke, the reservationist shook her head from side to side, the woman shrugged happily, hopped on her bike and left – we could tell that she had been denied a reservation.

My sixth sense was speaking to me, telling me that something wasn't right. I sent Ariel over to see what had happened. He returned and informed me that she was looking for a table for four for eight o'clock.

'And?' I asked.

'The girl told her that we were fully –'

I realised who it was: 'Jesus Christ, Ariel, that was Jacqueline Kennedy Onassis.'

He considered that for a moment.

'Oh my God, Pino! You're right!'

I pointed to the highway. 'Go after her!'

Ariel's jaw dropped, but he didn't move.

'We cannot allow this to happen. Go!'

'Pino, she's gone down the highway.'

'So go chase her down the fucking highway! This cannot happen. Not here!'

With a shrug, Ariel began walking towards the road.

'You're not going to get her if you walk. Run!'

Ariel began running in his immaculate white linen suit, slipping his jacket off as he started. Our driveway was covered with gravel, so he couldn't really pick up any speed until he got to the highway.

I went out to the edge of my property and looked down the sloping highway. I could see the former First Lady about half a mile down the road, stopped at an intersection, straddling her bike, and behind her, coming up fast, my own Latin Gatsby, running down the road after her to gallantly offer her a table.

She was about to start pedalling again, but he called out to her and she stopped and turned round. They spoke. She nodded and he waved goodbye.

Ariel returned to our parking lot, drenched in sweat. He reported his success. She had accepted the reservation and his apology.

I was so happy. I had always admired Jackie O. Not just her style, but also her strength after her husband was assassinated and all those stories about how she had raised her children, Caroline and John, Jr., to be humble and polite. She clearly lived those values herself. I mean, here she was in the Hamptons, where *everyone* wants you to know who they are, and she didn't even divulge her identity to get a table at a restaurant.

I had to compliment Ariel on his triumph: 'I'm proud of you, Ariel. You did what the best maître d' in the Hamptons should do, and you should feel good about it.'

He nodded, still catching his breath and fanning himself off. 'Thanks, Pino.'

I looked him up and down. Sweat was literally dripping off his suit.

'Now, go take a shower,' I said. 'You stink!'

I'm telling you, our work is *never* done.

What do you eat for breakfast?
My favourite breakfast item is eggs, prepared in any way possible.

What dish would you cook in order to seduce someone?
Two eggs easy over, with melted Fontina cheese and white truffles. This dish will seduce anyone . . .

What do you never cook?
French food.

What do you find hard to get right?
Anything that takes more than an hour from beginning to end and any dish that requires more than five ingredients.

You Really Ought to
Think about Becoming a Waiter

ERIC RIPERT

In 1995, as executive chef of Le Bernardin, Eric Ripert became one of an elite group of chefs to earn four stars from the New York Times. *Prior to arriving at Le Bernardin, he studied at the culinary institute in Perpignan and worked at some of the world's finest restaurants, including Paris's La Tour D'Argent and Jamin and also Jean-Louis at the Watergate Hotel in Washington, DC. He is the author of* Le Bernardin Cookbook *and* A Return to Cooking.

MOST AMERICAN CHEFS I know have never considered becoming a waiter, not even for a second. But there comes a moment in every French cooking student's life when he has to make a crucial decision: 'Am I going to become a chef or am I going to become a waiter?'

They have to make this decision because French culinary schools insist that you spend time learning to be a front-of-house professional as well as a cook. For this reason, many of my classmates not only considered becoming waiters, they actually did become waiters.

I never wanted to be a waiter. I had always had a passion for eating and cooking, so had dreamt of becoming a chef since I was a little kid. But I almost became a waiter anyway. In fact, if it weren't for the day that my mother came to lunch at our school's restaurant, I might be a waiter now.

When I was fifteen years old, I enrolled in the culinary institute in Perpignan, a town of about 100,000 people in the South of France. Perpignan was the closest serious cooking school to my home of Andorra, a co-principality on the southern slope of the Pyrenees between France and Spain, approximately three and a half hours away by car. The school had a three-year course for younger kids and a more intensive, two-year course for guys like me. It also offered training in hairdressing and nursing, so it wasn't a bad place for a fifteen-year-old boy to find himself for two years.

Though situated in an ancient town, the school was contemporary in every way, with modern, meticulously maintained buildings, state-of-the-art classrooms and kitchen equipment, and a handsome little restaurant where we were able to practise our trade on real customers.

The school had an interesting history: many of the instructors had previously cooked or served aboard the legendary French luxury liner *Le France*. Once the pride of the nation, *Le France* had been so grossly mismanaged that the government-owned ship was permanently docked. Its last port of call was Perpignan, and many of the chefs, cooks and waiters stayed in the town, becoming instructors at the school.

All of my teachers were very knowledgeable and very strict, after a 1950s model of discipline, discipline, discipline. They treated us like cadets in a military academy, like the crew of their own landlocked ship: you didn't question their authority, *ever*. If you did, or if you screwed up badly enough, you might find a sauté pan hurled at you. Adding to this military air was the classic uniform that the 300 to 400 culinary students wore: crisp white apron and jacket, a toque, and a white neckerchief. A kitchen team is called a *brigade*, and that's what we looked like: an army of cooks.

As with any French culinary school, we devoted just as much time to learning about the dining room as we did to learning about the culinary arts. We spent two days a week serving customers in the school's student-operated restaurant, two days in the kitchen, and one day in the classroom studying the fundamentals of cuisine, as well as management, accounting, and other related topics.

The kitchen was a tough place and it required great patience. Just like a piano student needs to learn notes before he can play scales, and then tunes, a culinary student starts with the basics. And the basics can be pretty tedious. The first thing I remember learning to do was clean the stove, and I wasn't even the one who had dirtied it.

In the dining room, however, you got to the heart of the work straight away. And you didn't just wait at tables, you also learnt how to debone ducks and chickens, fillet fish, and perform such flamboyant acts as flambéing, so if you still had a desire to cook, you got to do a little of that, too.

More important, choice was limited, so while the school-masters would try to accommodate your wish, it was simply a mathematical fact that some students were going to end up in the dining room.

There was an additional factor, too, one that might be difficult to comprehend: whereas in many countries waiting tables is a way for out-of-work actors or unskilled labourers to pay the rent, in France, it's a proud profession with a noble history. Accordingly, the dining-room instructors were just as passionate about their work as the chef instructors were about theirs. So becoming a waiter began to look very appealing to some of the guys, especially when they found themselves ducking a flying sauté pan.

No single person inspired more people to become waiters at the Perpignan culinary institute than the tough-but-fair manager-instructor of the school's restaurant, Monsieur Moccan. He was like a Dickens character: well into his forties, he was a chubby, slightly hunchbacked, bespectacled figure who strode through the dining room greeting customers with one voice and using another, stronger, firmer voice to correct any mistakes in his path.

Monsieur Moccan thought I was the best waiter in my class, and he took every opportunity to tell me so. He tried to push me, more than anyone, out to the front of the house for the rest of my life.

But I never changed my answer: I wanted to work in the kitchen.

Towards the end of my first year of school, a decision had to be made about what the focus of my second year, and consequently my career, would be. Of course, my mind was made up, but I was only sixteen, and they wanted me in the dining room, so it was decided that my mother and stepfather would make the drive from Andorra, have lunch in our restaurant, and meet the administrators to discuss my future.

To make the day as special as possible, and afford me an opportunity to impress my family, Monsieur Moccan appointed me sommelier for the afternoon. The thought was that, with nothing to do put pour wine and shuttle cocktails from the bar to the tables, an accomplished waiter like me would have an easy time of it and put a big smile on Mum's face.

I donned the waiter's uniform (white jacket with epaulettes, bow tie, black trousers, black socks, and leather shoes), and the shift began uneventfully. I walked the medium-sized room, surveying the hundred or so seats, just as comfortable as I always was.

As the lunch service progressed and the dining room filled to capacity, a *real* military man came into our little academy: a colonel from the French army, about sixty years old, rather skinny, in uniform, with his wife and a civilian couple. I took their cocktail orders, got the drinks from the barman and returned with one of our round, rimmed drinks trays balanced on my open palm. Before I could get one glass on the table, something happened that had never happened before: I lost control of the tray, turning all four drinks over on the colonel and soaking his beautiful starched uniform.

To his credit, the colonel didn't lose his composure. He wasn't happy, but he was a true gentleman about my mistake and he sat there patiently while I patted his back dry.

Monsieur Moccan hurried over to the scene of the disaster and pulled me aside, supportive as ever. 'Don't get stressed. The guy's going to be OK. He's knows it's the restaurant of the school.' But he was also just as firm as he always was. 'Go and fill up your tray again, come back, and serve them,' he instructed. 'You have to finish the job.'

So I got the drinks again and came back as fast as I could. It turns out I came back too fast because they hadn't had a chance to clean the floor. As I approached the colonel's wife, I slipped on the ice cubes from the first disaster and upended the tray on her. I expected her to start screaming, but I think they were all in shock at this point. Nobody said a word to me as I did my best to clean the table and help her dry herself off.

Once again, Monsieur Moccan began whispering in my ear, telling me to go back to the bar and finish the job. I remember thinking that I hadn't even started it yet.

When I returned to the bar, the barman looked at me as though he had just found out I had six weeks to live – his eyes conveyed pity, sadness, and discomfort. With a sigh, he replenished my tray once again and I gingerly made my way back to my little table of horrors. *En route*, I noticed that a quarter-inch of water had collected in the well of the tray. Convinced that lightning couldn't possibly strike three times, and unwilling to lose any more time before successfully serving the table their drinks, I resolved simply to be careful and leave the water where it was. I delivered three of the drinks without incident, then turned to the colonel. He nodded slightly to me. I nodded in return. And as I reached for his drink, the tray tipped, spilling the water in his face.

That was it. The colonel shot up out of his chair and began screaming, 'That's enough! Get this person out of here!'

I flinched, taking a few nervous backward steps. But he wasn't yelling at me. He was yelling at Monsieur Moccan, who was suddenly nowhere to be found – until I spotted him through the little window in the kitchen door, laughing uncontrollably, unable to compose himself and return to the dining room.

'As for *you* . . .' the colonel shouted at me. And I stood there while he dressed me down in full view of the customers, who watched in awe, my mother slowly turning green, struggling to understand why the school so desperately wanted her son to become a waiter.

I never did manage to spend time at my mother's table that day, and I'm sure I didn't impress her, especially with where I ended up next: demoted to dishwasher. But at least I had found my way back to the kitchen, and I never came out again.

––––––––––

What do you eat for breakfast?
Greek yoghurt and honey.

What dish would you cook in order to seduce someone?
Anything with truffles.

What do you never cook?
Brains.

What's the one dish you find hard to get right?
None.

On the Road Again
DANIEL BOULUD

Originally from Lyon, Daniel Boulud is one of the most acclaimed chefs in New York City. His empire includes the four-star dining temple Daniel, as well as Café Boulud and DB Bistro Moderne. Trained under some of the legendary chefs of France, Boulud made his name as the executive chef of the Polo Lounge and Le Cirque, before opening his own restaurants. He is the author of several cookbooks and the designer of the Daniel Boulud Kitchen line of cookware.

W E CHEFS FREQUENTLY find ourselves practising our craft away from our own restaurants, whether for one of the seemingly nightly benefit events in New York City, at private affairs or television appearances or book signings.

Whenever you leave your own carefully calibrated kitchen – a facility that each chef tailors and tweaks to his own ever-changing needs and specifications – there is a risk. Away from your home base, variables abound: the setting and infrastructure, the support staff, the kitchen equipment, even the serving dishes can cause unforeseen problems.

Out-of-house disasters are funny to look back on, but only because they usually end well. I bet if you ask chefs for their best stories from the road, they all wrap up with the food on the table and the customers having no idea of the chaos that transpired behind the scenes. There's a very simple reason for this: *in my business, failure is not an option.* The mark of a professional is that, no matter what happens, no matter how catastrophic the circumstances, you complete your job on time and to your standards and those of your guests.

To minimise the chance of a disaster, many chefs transport, even fly, their own ingredients to event sites. But sometimes this is impractical, like the time I was in Tel Aviv to do a gala dinner for 200 with Norman Van Aken, Thomas Keller, Nobu Matsuhisa, and Toronto's Susser Lee. Susser was going to prepare a stuffed quail, but when the quail appeared, at two o'clock on the afternoon of the dinner, boneless, limp, and corroded by kosherising salt, I saw before me a man in crisis.

It was a truly terrible situation. Nobu, Thomas, Norman and I wanted to jump in and help, but Susser had to completely change gear and didn't have time to collaborate. He ordered the support staff just to 'bring me stuff, bring me stuff', in the hope that some new ingredients would spark his imagination. And they did: by dinnertime, he had pulled off a lovely duck dish. The happy guests had no idea that anything had gone wrong.

Equipment is another fertile breeding ground for trouble. I

once did a dinner at a major New York museum, in a room that had no stoves, and which was forbidden by building regulations from having any gas or electric machines brought in. One of my new cooks, looking for a way to reroast the meat dish, put fifteen to twenty cans of sterno under a sheet pan in an enclosed wooden cabinet. When we opened the cabinet door, we were greeted by a fireball; the heat was so intense – easily in excess of 700 degrees – that the sheet pan had started to melt.

But the most difficult element to control is people, especially those you didn't hire and who will only be working with you for one day. For example, one of the most heart-stopping things that ever happened to me involved the most unlikely worker: a truck driver.

The year was 1989. I was chef at Le Cirque, Sirio Maccioni's restaurant. Malcolm Forbes had famously decided to throw himself a seventieth-birthday party in Morocco, and in order to transport his 700 American guests, including such legends as Henry Kissinger and Barbara Walters, he chartered two private 747s and a Concorde to fly out of Kennedy Airport.

Le Cirque was enlisted to prepare a four-star breakfast for the flights. We spared no expense, purchasing elegant little baskets and preparing individual meals of our own bread, a hard-boiled egg, sausage, Evian, orange juice, linen napkins, and so on.

To ensure the food was maintained at ultimate freshness, we hired a refrigerated truck the night before the flight. We prepped food well into the wee hours, then loaded the truck and instructed the driver to sleep in his seat and keep the truck parked outside the restaurant. We would return in the morning and head to the airport with him to present the food.

We went home at two in the morning, got a few hours' sleep, and came back at six-thirty . . . only to find that the truck had disappeared.

If this story had happened today, the first thing I would have done was whip out my cell phone and call the driver on his. But this was in 1989. Almost nobody had a cell phone – except for Sirio, who owned one roughly the size of a man's shoe.

Once we recovered from the shock of the missing truck, we decided that perhaps the driver had misunderstood and gone to the airport. We piled into a car and made for JFK, with Sirio frantically calling anyone on the planet who might be able to solve this problem.

At the airport, hundreds of Malcolm Forbes's guests, a who's who of New York society, were filing into a private hangar that had been converted into a Moroccan lounge, with decorations, live music, even a belly dancer. There was everything you could imagine.

But not a single scrap of food, and no truck in sight.

At this point, I thought Sirio might actually kill somebody. And I'll be honest: I didn't know what we were going to do.

Well, everyone is entitled to a little luck and that was the morning when I got mine. At the last possible second, the truck came barrelling down the runway and we just managed to get the food served to the guests, who had by then taken their seats on board the planes. It turned out that the driver had gone home and overslept, with the most famous breakfast on earth parked outside in his driveway.

*   *   *

One place you don't ever get lucky is in the kitchen. You either make the food right or you don't. Without a doubt, my biggest challenge came on a day when we *had* made the food right, but it was undone by the on-site staff.

This was in the mid-nineties. I was still operating out of the original Daniel space on East Seventy-sixth Street, and I was enlisted to be the culinary chairman of a rain-forest benefit, a seated dinner for 1,000 people that followed a concert by Elton John and Sting. I had complete creative control of the three courses we were to serve, except for one: they insisted that the first course be a pea soup featured on my restaurant menu at the time.

We didn't have the capacity to cook on that scale in my restaurant's kitchen, so we planned to do it at the hotel, enlisting the help of the on-site staff.

Just as it is in a home kitchen, one of the crucial concerns of making pea soup is chilling it as soon as it's been cooked, to prevent it from turning brown and to keep the vegetables from fermenting.

I love logistical challenges like this so I had already sat down with my calculator and notepad and determined how many batches we'd have to make to end up with 1,200 servings, the 1,000 for which we were contracted, plus a 20 per cent contingency. I had also devised a system of keeping the soup chilled that involved storing it in batches in a number of 25-gallon stainless-steel containers set in ice water, and periodically stirring it to distribute the chilled portion within the canister and help bring down the overall temperature of the batch.

We made the soup the day before the event, then left the site, entrusting it to the hotel's kitchen staff. They were supposed to keep the canisters in the cooler, in regularly replenished ice water, and stir the soup every hour. As far as I can tell, when the shift changed in the mid-afternoon, the new guys didn't give a damn and just left the canisters sitting there, completely unattended.

At the end of the day, I dispatched a few guys from my kitchen to check on the status of things at the hotel. When they entered the refrigerator to inspect the soup, there was greenish-yellow-brown foam bubbling over the tops of the canisters.

Though the soup had undoubtedly fermented, this is one of those evaluations that only the chef can make, so my guys ladled a sample of the soup into a plastic container and had it shuttled up to me at Daniel. As soon as I saw it, I could tell it was gone, and a taste made this all too clear: the soup, all 1,200 servings worth, was sour, useless garbage.

At that moment, the event – for me and my team – became more of a military operation than a culinary endeavour. I outlined a rigorous plan that began with the guys on site pouring the spoilt soup down the drain and ended with 1,000 guests enjoying a perfect soup the next evening.

OK, now here's the amazing thing about a crisis like this: the actual cooking was the *second* concern. The first concern was replenishing the supplies required to make that much soup, most notably about 400 lbs of a variety of five peas. I called every purveyor I could think of, then one of my cooks, and I got in a van and personally drove around town, starting in Harlem and working our way south, buying up all the peas we could find.

As for the stock, even if we could have put our hands on enough bones to make a new one from scratch, it didn't matter, because there wasn't time for it patiently to simmer. Fortunately I know how to work with a powdered stock base if I have to.

Instead of making the entire soup hot and chilling it, we used a few kitchen tricks to save time, blanching and chilling the peas, chilling the stock separately, then combining the two. We also used a complicated series of shallow vessels set in ice water to keep it as cold as possible.

When it was time to serve the soup, 1,000 little bowls came marching out of the kitchen, beautifully garnished with rosemary-infused cream and rosemary croutons, and little bowls of bacon crackling on the side for anyone who wanted it.

Just the way it was always meant to be.

What do you eat for breakfast?
Granola or muesli with milk or yoghurt and fresh fruit, unless I am travelling in France – in which case I cannot resist a croissant.

What dish would you cook in order to seduce someone?
The inspiration would be different for each season, but now it's the height of black-truffle season so my menu would be smooth, creamy scrambled eggs with plenty of fresh black truffle, served for breakfast in bed, of course.

What do you never cook?
Anything with bananas.

What's the one dish you find hard to get right?

If you are well organised, have excellent ingredients and the equipment, staff and time you need, there is little that can't be done. But I must admit I had a difficult time with *poulet en vessie* (a whole chicken poached in a pig's bladder) for a 300-person gala wine-tasting dinner. When the chicken is perfectly done, the bladder puffs up into a balloon and must be served at just the right moment to get the full effect of the very spectacular presentation. I don't recommend trying this at home for a large group, but for me it's hard to pass up a challenge.

Ship of Fools
JIMMY BRADLEY

Jimmy Bradley co-owns and operates a number of New York City restaurants that started out as neighbourhood joints and wound up as destinations for diners from across the country: the Red Cat, the Harrison, the Mermaid Inn, and (the more grand-scaled) Pace. After attending the University of Rhode Island, Bradley worked in some of Philadelphia and Rhode Island's top kitchens before becoming executive chef of Savoir Fare, a progressive Martha's Vineyard bistro where he began his trade-mark style of straightforward, boldly flavoured seasonal cooking.

THIS STORY WOULD never happen today. It probably could only have taken place in the 1980s, when drug and alcohol abuse in the restaurant industry were at their zenith. The names of the restaurant, the chef, and the owner have been changed to protect the innocent, the not-so-innocent, and – most importantly – myself.

In 1986, I was a young cook working in a seaside resort town along the coast of Rhode Island, not unlike the kind of place you might find along the Jersey Shore. I worked for a restaurant – we'll call it the Harbor Cove Inn – that was one of the better eateries in the area, one of the few places that didn't make its money on an autopilot menu of baked scrod with Ritz cracker crumbs, lobster Newburg, and baked stuffed shrimp.

The Harbor Cove Inn was as close to fine dining as it got in this town: a nondescript, carpeted dining room; walls papered with parchment; a staff of salty locals, high-school students, and college kids; and a small but serviceable kitchen in the back.

Credit for our noteworthy offerings belonged to the chef – we'll call him Fernando – a Puerto Rican who had worked in New York City and, through some cruel twist of fate that I never really understood, wound up in this tiny hamlet. I liked Fernando. He was talented, both creatively and as a kitchen technician. And he liked me, enough that he promoted me from line cook to sous-chef in a very short time.

The third character in this ill-fated tale is the restaurant's owner, a Rhode Island wise guy who for our purposes will go by the name of Frankie. You've seen men like Frankie in the movies, or on *The Sopranos* – connected guys who have their hands in a mix of local businesses. Frankie owned not only a restaurant but also an auto dealership and a liquor store, and he was on the board of just about every committee in town. Like those movie and TV characters, Frankie had a base of operations, an office in a huge complex, where he ran his empire, his only visible aid coming from the 'girl' at the secretary station outside his office, a sweet, maternal figure named (not really) Delores.

Frankie was a real local character. He might not have stood out much in New York or New Jersey, but in this little Rhode Island town his three-piece suits combined with his diminutive stature and bruiser's gait made it easy to spot him from a mile away – as did his hair, which, though he was only in his mid- to late thirties, was prematurely grey.

I had been working at the Harbor Cove Inn for eight or nine months when, one February day, a ray of sunshine broke upon my bleak New England winter. Frankie strutted into the restaurant and, apropos of nothing, pulled aside me and Fernando. 'Listen,' he told us, 'I just saw this new space that's up for grabs. I think we could do something really nice there. You guys can have some more creative freedom, the town'll get another good restaurant, and we'll all make some more money. Everybody's gonna win.'

Fernando and I couldn't have been more excited. We drove over to check out the space and discovered, to our delight, a charming little converted house with enough space between its white clapboard walls and the street to allow for outdoor seating in the spring and summer. Inside, the dining room had space enough to accommodate comfortably about 100 people – significantly more than the Harbor Cove – and a bar from which we could already imagine the flow of white Zinfandels and Fuzzy Navels, the drinks of the moment in 1980s Rhode Island beach towns.

We headed straight back to the Harbor Cove and started making up dishes for the new place – doing our thing with lobster, filet mignon and veal – running them as nightly specials starting that very day.

Over the next four months, we did everything in our power to ensure that, when the restaurant opened in the summer, it would make a big splash – continuing to evolve those dishes, designing the kitchen, and so on.

Come summertime, Frankie planned a big opening party for the new restaurant. We had what was supposed to be our last meeting a week before the party, but on the day of the party, Frankie abruptly summoned us to another meeting. When we arrived, Fernando and I were in sky-high spirits, chattering about how much fun we were going to have that night.

And then, Frankie threw a big wet blanket over the two of us. 'Listen, fellas,' he said, 'the rest of the investors and I talked it over and we decided that, since this is really an invite-only party, you two shouldn't be there.'

It took a moment for this to sink in. After all, how could the chef and sous-chef not attend the opening of the restaurant they'd just spent four months getting ready? Did it mean we were being fired? I glanced over at Fernando, who looked equally worried.

'Shouldn't *one* of us be there?' Fernando said, taking a shot at an appeal.

Frankie shook his little grey head.

'No. You guys did a great job getting the food ready, but I really need you to stay back at the Harbor Cove Inn and make sure things run smoothly there tonight.'

Heads hanging low, and wondering if our livelihoods were at stake – not to mention feeling considerably insulted – we returned to the Harbor Cove Inn and did what cooks do: our jobs, sullenly starting to prep for that evening's service. In an attempt to take my mind off the situation, I turned on the radio I kept at my station, and even started making a big vat of spaghetti sauce for the next day, stirring it with a long, paddle-like wand as it simmered away.

But Fernando was consumed with anger. For the next hour, I watched it boil up within him. He didn't say a word, but everything he did was fuelled by fury. When he'd put a sauté pan to the flame, he'd bang it down like he was clubbing someone over the head. When he'd cut a cucumber, he'd bring the knife down so hard I was sure he was picturing Frankie's neck there on his cutting board.

One thing was certain: if Fernando didn't get a grip, this was going to be a long night.

Less than an hour before service, Fernando was still stomping around, slamming refrigerator doors and flinging pans into the sink. The kitchen staff were on edge and the waiters were nervously keeping their distance. I took it upon myself to perform an intervention.

'Chef, what're we gonna do about this? We gotta find a way to chill out.'

Fernando ignored me, continuing his sadistic vivisection of yet another hapless vegetable. But then, suddenly, he was gripped with inspiration. He put down his knife, turned, and looked me in the eye. 'Fuck this!' he said. 'You wanna know what the fuck we're gonna do? I'll tell you what the fuck we're gonna do!'

I stepped back, thinking, Oh shit. This ain't gonna be good.

Fernando was possessed with a dark clarity that, if it weren't so scary, would have been impressive. He began barking orders to the kitchen staff: '*You*, go get me a bucket. *You*, go get me three bottles of vodka and two bottles of triple sec. *You*, go get a big mess of limes and squeeze 'em, and bring me the juice. *You*, bring me some ice.'

Those of us who weren't scattered about to do Fernando's bidding stood there in rapt anticipation, watching our commander-in-chief, wondering where this was all headed.

'And *me*,' he said, the glimmer in his eye approaching supernova status, 'I'm gonna stand here and make five gallons worth of shots.'

Shots? So he was going to get hammered? Big deal.

If only that were the case.

Fernando wasn't just going to get himself hammered. He had devised a new drinking game for the express entertainment of the staff of the Harbor Cove Inn. He summoned the entire crew – the waiters, the bartenders, the busboys, the dishwashers, and the cooks – and began to explain the rules. Normally, the maître d' would've stepped in and put a stop to this, but – guess what? – he was invited to the party. The cat was away, so to speak.

'Listen up,' Fernando said to us. 'I've come to a decision and I feel strongly about it. This is what's going to happen tonight: if you are going to perform any duty that has anything to do with fulfilling your job, then before you do that duty, you *must* do a shot. So, bartenders, if you're going to make a drink, you do a shot. Busboys, if you're going to clear a table, you do a shot. Waiters, before you take a tray of food to a table, you do a shot. Dishwashers, before you take a rack out of the steamer, you do a shot.'

We were all taken aback by this scheme, but before we could say a word in protest, Fernando cemented the deal.

'OK. Right now. Everybody, let's do a shot. Come on!'

We obeyed our orders, even the fresh-faced kids, and knocked back a shot. Then we got into positions for the first guests.

I must admit that much of that evening is a blur to me. It was like being on a ship that was rocking to and fro; we were doing our best just to stay on our feet, wobbling and weaving and fighting occasional bouts of nausea, yet somehow, miraculously, maintaining verticality.

As the evening wore on, Fernando got more and more aggressive with the game. Doing a shot became part of his commands: 'We need some more sauté pans over here. Bring me some sauté pans *and do a shot*.' 'Table Twelve is ready. Pick up Table Twelve *and do a shot*.'

By eight-thirty, the kitchen was inundated with orders, and struggling to work through. Fernando, though drunk, had enough presence of mind to know that we were at the point of no return. He once again summoned the entire staff into the kitchen, including the front-of-house team.

With everyone assembled, dizzily listing to one side, or leaning on each other for balance, Fernando continued his fierce display of leadership. 'OK, guys. We're almost there. One last big push and we're through the night. I know you can all do it . . . so let's do a shot and keep on going.'

As we all did yet another shot, Fernando came over to my station and turned the radio up full blast. The kitchen was flooded with the theme song of *Hawaii Five-O: Buh buh buh buh buh buh. Ba puh puh puh puh*.

Fernando took the wand out of my hand and began rowing an imaginary canoe.

. . . *buh buh buh buh buh buh* . . .

He did it with such gusto that I joined in, paddling in synch with the music and my fearless leader . . .

. . . *bah puh puh puh puh* . . .

One by one, the entire staff joined in, grabbing paddles, and when those ran out, tongs, spatulas, wooden spoons, anything that would get the idea across.

I later learnt that, unbeknownst to us, at about the time Fernando was giving us his pep talk, Frankie had returned to the Harbor Cove Inn from his party. He had walked in through the front door and seen a dining room full of customers, with not one staff member in sight. No coffee was being poured, no bread was being served, no dirty plates were being cleared – just a lot of confused diners wondering what the hell was going on.

And at the moment that we were all hopping on board the incredible, invisible canoe, Frankie had come into the kitchen, witnessed the spectacle for himself, and slipped back out. Amazingly, he went unnoticed by the entire drunken lot of us.

The next day, I managed to find my way back to the Harbor Cove Inn. Fernando, professional that he was, was already there. Also on hand was the general manager, who had been at the party the night before. We didn't know why, but the manager gave us the cold shoulder all morning. What's *his* problem, I wondered. *He* got to go to the party.

Later that morning, we got a call from Delores, Frankie's secretary, informing us that Frankie wanted us to come to his office for a meeting.

Fernando and I smiled at each other. Surely, we thought, we were being summoned over for a belated apology for the party slight.

We drove to the complex that housed Frankie's office and took the elevator up to his suite. As always, Delores was sitting at the desk outside.

'Hi ya, boys, how ya doin'?'

'Great, Delores. You?'

'OK, I guess.'

'What's Frankie want?'

'I don't know. He wouldn't say. But go on in. He's ready for you.'

Fernando and I exchanged a wry smile and I opened the door to Frankie's office, a huge, spartan room with wraparound picture windows that offered a spectacular view of the Atlantic.

Frankie had one of those old-fashioned, high-backed leather executive chairs and, when we entered the room, he was seated in it, facing the ocean. We couldn't see him at all. As we sat on the couch in front of the desk, we found ourselves staring at this monolithic wall of leather.

We waited in silence for what felt like a week. Frankie didn't make a sound, just let us sit there, wondering what was coming.

Finally, he spun around in the chair. His face was purple with anger. He stood up and leaned forward against the desk, putting the palms of his hands on the shiny black surface for support, and stared us both right in the eyes. But he didn't say a word. Instead, he picked up the newspaper and walked around to our side of the desk. Then he tossed the paper at our chests and sauntered out the door.

Fernando and I looked at each other in bewilderment, then down at the paper. Staring back at us was the 'Help Wanted' section, opened to the page featuring restaurants and bars.

'Are we fired?' I asked Fernando.

'I don't know.'

We left the office and found Delores parked at her desk.

'Hey, Delores, are we fired?'

'Yeah. I'm sorry, boys. Frankie just told me on the way out. He said to have you escorted out of the building, and to tell you that he'd like to never see either of you again.'

I've been in the restaurant business for close to twenty years.

That was the first time I was fired, and – since I own my own places now – probably the last.

Fernando doesn't own his own restaurants, but the two of us found work just two days later in another fine restaurant about five miles away from Frankie's joint, and Fernando's still working there to this day. So even though we haven't spoken in years, I like to think that he looks back on that night with humour and some measure of pride, for giving us one hell of an evening to look back on . . . even if we can't remember many of the details.

What do you eat for breakfast?
Bloody Marys and Marlboros or toast with butter, sugar and cinnamon.

What dish would you cook in order to seduce someone?
French fries and pink champagne.

What do you never cook?
Calves' liver.

What's the one dish you find hard to get right?
Blue-cheese gougère.

Beastmaster
WYLIE DUFRESNE

From Providence, Rhode Island, Wylie Dufresne studied philosophy at Colby College before enrolling at the French Culinary Institute in New York City. Following graduation, he spent several years working for Jean-Georges Vongerichten, first at JoJo, then at the four-star Jean-Georges, and finally as chef de cuisine of Vongerichten's Prime in Las Vegas. In 1999, he was opening chef at 71 Clinton Fresh Food, where his father was a partner, on New York's Lower East Side, the same neighbourhood that plays home to his first restaurant, wd-50. Dufresne was nominated for the James Beard Foundation award for Rising Star Chef in 2000, and in 2001 he was named one of Food & Wine Magazine's best new chefs.

I'M A MEMBER of perhaps the last generation of American chefs who considered it essential to spend at least a few weeks cooking in France early in their careers. While many of today's kitchen hopefuls feel they can learn all they need to know here at home in the United States, it was different for me and my contemporaries. Whereas liberal-arts students might have taken a postgraduate month to backpack around Europe, *culinary* school grads went to Europe to cook, usually for little or no money, and to see how things were done in the birthplace of Western cuisine.

I didn't make it to France right out of cooking school. I hadn't even made it there by the time I was twenty-six.

I had my reasons. I had spent the past few years working at JoJo for Jean-Georges Vongerichten, one of the most talented, respected, and influential chefs in the country. Today, Jean-Georges operates restaurants all over the US and the world. But in the mid-90s, he had a mere two, JoJo and Vong, so working at one of them meant working alongside this master. It was an exciting, wonderful, glorious place for a young cook to be, and I made the most of it, spending time at every station in the kitchen.

In 1996, my mentor was putting the finishing touches on what would become his four-star masterpiece, the self-titled Restaurant Jean-Georges, situated in the Trump International Hotel on Columbus Circle in New York City. Though he wasn't fond of moving employees from one place to another, I felt like I had gotten all I was going to get out of JoJo, and asked him if he might consider transferring me to Jean-Georges when it opened. He agreed, offering me the job of *saucier*.

I then made another request: I wanted to take the month of November, between leaving my position at JoJo and the opening of Jean-Georges, and finally fulfil my long-delayed rite of passage by travelling to France and working in a three-star Michelin kitchen, a learning period of temporary employment commonly referred to as a *stage*.

Jean-Georges's response blew me away. Not only could I have the time off, but he would arrange for me to work at Alain Passard's Michelin three-star Arpege, his favourite restaurant of the moment. Passard was renowned for minimalist dishes that had just three or four elements on the plate and *nothing* else. What an amazing place it would be to hone my technique. And to go there with Jean-Georges's seal of approval was just too much. It was going to be the best experience of my life!

At least that's what I, at the time, naively, happily imagined. I never did discover the joys of Arpege because in all the hubbub of running JoJo, on the jam-packed heels of its *second* three-star review no less, and readying Restaurant Jean-Georges, acting as my overseas agent somehow fell off Jean-Georges's monumental agenda. At the time I was crestfallen, but now that I'm a chef myself, I must say that I can completely understand how it happened.

Two days before my departure, the team at Jean-Georges scrambled to line up a job for me at Mark Meneau, the eponymous Michelin three-star restaurant of a member of the old guard of French gastronomy, a master chef who had never attained the celebrity of his peers like Paul Bocuse or the Troisgros brothers, but who was very well respected. In his fifties at the time, Meneau was a true scholar of classic French cuisine, who would often refer his cooks to recipes in *L'Escoffier*, providing the page number to them from his frighteningly accurate memory.

So, rather than staying in Paris when I got off the plane, I boarded a train at Gare du Nord and travelled deep into the heart of Burgundy. A taxi took me even further into the region, shuttling me through the pretty French countryside towards the town of Saint-Père-sous-Vézelay, where I was delivered, at last, to the door of Mark Meneau.

It was everything that I expected it would be: a small restaurant on one side of the narrow road and a large banquet hall – that seemed to have a capacity double the size of the town's modest population – on the other.

Though a bit disheartened that I wasn't in Paris, I was excited to have a crack at the three-star experience. I was also determined to represent myself and Jean-Georges as well as possible. I resolved to be on time every day, and to do my level best to keep pace with what I expected to be my competition: fifteen-year-old French punks who had cooking in their blood and could do everything twice as well and twice as fast as a lowly American like myself.

I needn't have worried about receiving a chilly reception, however. I was warmly taken in by the kitchen staff, who assigned me, not surprisingly, to the *garde manger* (salads and cold appetisers) station, a frequent destination for newcomers to a kitchen because it involves no actual cooking, other than maybe blanching and shocking vegetables, though I was – as feared – working alongside three French teenagers who were also performing a *stage*.

The kitchen was magnificent, reason enough to have made the long trip. After working in JoJo's functional but necessarily submarinelike quarters in a converted townhouse, it was revelatory to see what a chef would design when space simply wasn't an issue. Meneau's kitchen afforded everyone ease of movement from any point to any other point. There were separate walk-ins for dairy, meats, and so on. And there was meat hanging everywhere, being dried or aged to just the right effect. It was a model of French efficiency that I meticulously sketched before my two weeks were up. The dining room, too, was attractive and welcoming in a classic country Relais & Châteaux kind of way.

The restaurant managers were gracious enough to set me up in a little guesthouse about 100 yards down the road from the restaurant. The closer you got to the house, the more wooded and shadowy the road became. My room was at the end of a short, dark hallway on the second floor, which you reached by a spiral staircase with old-fashioned banisters. The house served as spillover accommodation for guests in the peak season, but it was nearly deserted in November, so much so that I was the only tenant on my floor.

It was at the end of that dark road, at the end of that empty hall, in a little room not much larger than a closet that I turned out the light and went to bed that first night, with urgent thoughts of punctuality occupying my last moment of consciousness. Tossing beneath the scratchy sheets, fighting off sleep, I ran through my morning routine one more time: wake up at eight-fifty, leap into the bathroom, shower, towel off, dress, grab my knives and my Carhartt jacket, and make the five-minute walk to the restaurant, arriving at nine o'clock sharp and doing Jean-Georges and my nation proud.

The first couple of days went well. I was on time each morning, kept my head down and focused intently on cleaning and slicing every vegetable that crossed my cutting board with the precision of a jeweller.

While I mostly kept to myself I did, however, strike up an acquaintance with the restaurant's baker. Or, rather *he* struck up an acquaintance with me, simply by directing an occasional smile my way or giving me a friendly pat on the back. Though an accomplished baker, he was a bit of an odd duck. He sat alone at lunch, and was the only member of the kitchen staff to drink a glass of wine with the meal. And in stark contrast to the other cooks in the kitchen, who wore immaculate starched whites, he rolled his pants up as if he were expecting a flood – his sleeves rolled up in similar country-bumpkin fashion.

So passed my first two days at Mark Meneau – not terribly social, but efficient and capable. I was meeting my goals and settling in nicely.

On my third morning, I awoke, showered, dressed, grabbed my knives and my Carhartt, and opened the door to leave.

From out of the darkness of the corridor, a shadowy figure emerged, blindingly fast, and whooshed past me into my room.

'What the fuck was that?' I said aloud, and spun around, following its trajectory.

Sitting there on my bed, eyes blinking as it surveyed my room, was an owl.

I'm a New York City kid, so I've seen my share of mice, pigeons, rats and other creatures that are indigenous to the island of Manhattan. I imagine there are owls in Central Park, but the only place I had ever seen one was on television, swooping down from the sky to grab some poor fish in its talons on the *National Geographic* show. I had never met one up close and personal.

Let me tell you something: owls are *huge*. And they seem even larger when they're parked on your bed in a dorm-room-sized hotel room.

I lost some time adjusting to the situation, but once I recovered, I remembered my vow never to be late for work. While my heart pounded furiously and sweat began pouring down my face, a glance at my watch revealed that I had about three minutes to make the trek.

Not knowing what else to do, I threw open the bedroom window and began gesturing at the owl, waving for it to avail itself of the exit.

Its blinking continued unabated.

I removed my Carhartt and took it in my hands like a bullfighter's cape. With a shooing motion, I tried to guide the owl towards the window, coming up around it from the side.

As I approached, it spread its wings wide like Dracula; in the heat of the moment, they appeared to fill the room. I backed off.

'Shoo,' I whispered meekly, then pleaded, 'C'mon, shoo.'

I'm not sure, but I think the owl yawned. Forget about my wishes; he seemed oblivious to my very existence.

Another glance at my watch: I had two minutes to get to work.

I left the window open, threw on my jacket, flew down the stairs, and sprinted the 100 yards to the restaurant, arriving in the nick of time, panting, my chest sore from sucking in the cold November air.

I worked all morning, preparing vegetables for lunch service. I also performed one of my favourite tasks, taking to the woods and foraging for perfect oak leaves that were laid out on plates at the restaurant, providing a rustically elegant surface on which cheeses were arranged.

After lunch service each day, we had a ninety-minute break. As soon as we were dismissed, I snuck off from the restaurant and made my way back to my little hotel room. I opened the door and was relieved to find that the owl was gone.

Or was he? He was nowhere in sight, but I needed proof. I checked the bathroom and behind the armchair. No owl. Then, more as a nod to what I had seen in the movies than to any real concern, I got on my knees and looked under the bed.

Sure enough, the owl was under the bed, blinking.

This is madness, I thought, as I left the room. I went back to the restaurant and sought out my lone acquaintance, the baker.

I found him seated at a table, eating his lunch and drinking his customary glass of wine. He greeted me with a nod.

I spoke to him using the dregs of my high-school French. I was able to communicate rather adroitly about cooking, but I had long forgotten the words and syntax that would enable me to explain the nature show that was going on in my bedroom – if I had ever learnt them in the first place.

In French, I said, '*I need you. To come. With me. To my room. My room. I need you to come to my room.*'

He cocked his head like a dog who knew you were giving him a command, but didn't know what it meant.

I began lurching my torso in the general direction of the guesthouse, to help make my point.

'*My room. I need you to come to my room. Come with me. With me.*'

I grabbed his arm, respectfully, to give him a sense of urgency.

'*Come with me to my room!*'

He shrugged, put down his wine glass, and stood up, indicating for me to lead the way.

We made the five-minute walk to the guesthouse in silence. I had no conversational French in my repertoire, and I don't think he was in a talking mood anyway.

Then it was up the stairs, down the dark corridor, and into my room. I gestured to the bed, talking in English now because I had no idea how to explain in French what needed doing.

'My bed. Look under my bed. Under the bed.'

He gave me a blank look.

Again, I resorted to physical contact, pulling him towards the bed. From the scowl on his face, I'm pretty sure that he thought I was trying to manoeuvre him *on to* the bed for the purposes of a between-meals tryst. But I managed to push him down close enough to the floor that when he looked *under* the bed he saw the owl.

The baker stood back up. I threw my hands in the air, as if to say, How the hell do you deal with a situation like this?

He gave me a pitying look, took one of the head posts of the bed in each hand, lifted one end of it off the floor, and the owl – as if this were a routine he and the baker did all the time – took off and flew out of the window.

The baker let the bed fall with a thud, turned on his heel and left the room, closing the door behind him.

He wasn't quite as friendly to me during my remaining week and a half at Mark Meneau. I did all right, though: in my second week, I was promoted to the hot line to fill in for a vacationing cook, leaving those young French kids in the dust. Then I took two weeks to explore Paris, before heading back home to New York and my new job in what remains one of the best restaurants in the city.

The French world for *owl*, by the way, is *chouette*, which also means 'cool' or 'brilliant'.

Yeah, right.

What do you eat for breakfast?
Peanut butter-and-banana milkshake that I make myself. (I've lost a lot of weight recently due to better eating and exercise.)

What dish would you cook in order to seduce someone?
I can't reveal that secret!

What do you never cook?
I rarely cook dinner for myself or friends.

What's the one dish you find hard to get right?
Countless things. We are currently working on hot ice cream and finding it particularly elusive; we've got it down to a soft-serve ice cream, but we are persisting with the consistency.

The Big Chill
MARCUS SAMUELSSON

The youngest chef ever to receive three stars from the New York Times, *and winner of the James Beard Foundation Award for Rising Star Chef in 1999 and Best Chef New York City in 2003, Marcus Samuelsson was born in Ethiopia, raised in Sweden, and trained all over the world before making Swedish food hip at Restaurant Aquavit in Midtown Manhattan. He is also an author of cookbooks in both Sweden and the United States.*

THE GLORIFICATION OF celebrity chefs has created the impression that my colleagues, and the cooks who work for us, spend our lives clowning around in the kitchen, then head off into the night, gallivanting around town and partying until dawn.

Sure, there are moments like that for any chef or cook, but generally speaking our work is more serious and taxing than most people realise. This is especially true of ambitious culinary students and novice cooks who lead disciplined, cruelly solitary existences that can be aptly compared to those of Olympic trainees or long-distance runners. They might blow off steam together after work, but for the most part their goal demands stamina of the mind and body and a single-minded devotion to their work. Without that sense of purpose, it's likely that they'd crack under the pressure, retreating from the industry or letting it destroy them.

I've seen guys crack in all kinds of ways. I once saw a cook so fatigued and distracted that he stuck his hand in a meat grinder and didn't get it out until four fingers were gone. I've seen good cooks driven to acts of self-destruction, going broke or turning to heroin. It's always the same: the pressure slowly builds, sometimes over several years, until they simply can't take it any more. They say, 'Fuck it,' and do something drastic and stupid.

Kitchen professionals are prone to breakdowns because nobody cares about their problems. At the end of the day, you're all alone. When you fuck up, nobody wants to know the reason; they just want to chew you out and leave you to pick up the pieces.

There have been many moments in my career when I myself was this close to throwing in the towel. Like when I worked for a cruise line and the *entremetier* (cook in charge of vegetable preparations), after months of smooth sailing, suddenly 'went down' – that is, fell victim to seasickness. Normally we'd have called the corporate headquarters and had a replacement cook flown in to meet us at our next port of call. But we were too far out to sea to orchestrate a switch. Like any true pro, the *entremetier* tried his best to hang in there, working himself so hard that he vomited, repeatedly, into a garbage can at his station. Finally we kicked him out, and in a gesture of camaraderie, attempted to cover for him by divvying up his dishes, one to the meat station, one to the fish station, and so on.

That didn't work. It's just too much to monitor the doneness of fifteen pieces of fish *and* sauté, say, some brussels sprouts to order – so even though the *entremetier* tried his best, and the rest of us were doing one and a half jobs each, all that mattered was whether or not the kitchen unit was getting the job done, and we weren't. Everybody, and I mean *everybody*, came into the kitchen to chew us out, including the captain of the ship itself.

You know that old expression, 'It's not whether you win or lose; it's how you play the game.' That line was definitely *not* coined by a chef. Because for a chef, it's *only* about whether or not you pull through. If you fail, nobody cares how hard you tried.

My loneliest, most discouraging professional moment came in the winter of 1988 when – thanks to the placement depart-ment of my culinary school – I was hired as a *commis* (lowest cook on the totem pole, a cog in the culinary machine) at La Terrasse, the fine dining room of the Victoria-Jungfrau hotel in Interlaken, Switzerland, an insanely ritzy hotel that catered to a mix of superwealthy Americans, Europeans, and Arabs, many of whom stayed for months at a time.

The kitchens of Victoria-Jungfrau in general, and La Terrasse in particular, had a reputation more or less comparable to that of the Navy Seals boot camp. The assumption was that they would break you and you would quit or be fired, and go crawling back to wherever you had come from. Turnover was so brisk that new students arrived every day, from places as far away as India and Japan. The upside was that those who survived were the best of the best, exactly the people you'd want to work with and learn from. And if you yourself could make it through all the hardships, then you'd be a better man, and a better cook.

Everybody had their own reasons for subjecting themselves to the rigours of this kitchen. I was there because I was eager to leave Sweden and cook at a three-star Michelin restaurant in France. But I was only eighteen and didn't feel ready yet, and thought that a turn in a place like La Terrasse would prepare me.

The setting was like something out of an opulent dream: a resort, more than a century old, set against the spectacular Jungfrau Mountain, where guests alternated between spa treatments, scenic hikes, and gourmet meals.

Days were long in the restaurant's huge kitchen. You worked all morning – me, at the *garde manger* (salads and cold appetisers) station – preparing and serving lunch, and also doing advance prep for dinner. The not-so-secret personal goal of each cook was to get your dinner prep done before lunch, so that, when the last lunch order was out, you could take a few hours off, either catching a nap in your little dormitory-sized room in the staff residence out back, or maybe sneaking in some skiing before returning for dinner service.

From the day I arrived, I led a very solitary existence at Victoria-Jungfrau. First of all, I don't think they had ever seen a black man in the kitchen before me. They sure as hell didn't expect one to show up when they hired a guy named Marcus Samuelsson from Sweden. But what can I tell you? I was born in Ethiopia, orphaned at a young age, and raised by a Swedish family. Anyway, it's my real name.

Then there was the language barrier. The chefs in that kitchen spoke German and French, a little English, and maybe a little Italian. I spoke none of those languages. This wasn't just a social handicap. Every morning, there was a kitchen meeting in which the executive chef, a real ogre in his sixties, reviewed the day's menu in German. I didn't understand him, and the printed menu, written in French, was of no use to me either. So I was dependent on my direct supervisor (the *chef de partie*, the person in charge of a station such as meat or fish, whom I refer to as '*my* chef') and colleagues to help me make sense of my work for the day after we left the meeting.

I had scarcely been there two weeks when New Year's Eve rolled along. As it is for any restaurant, New Year's Eve was one of the biggest nights of the year for La Terrasse, both for the diners and for the staff, who planned to work hard all day, then reward themselves by partying until dawn.

My chef and I were charged with making one dish that night: smoked salmon served with a thin sliver of avocado terrine. To make the terrine, you prepared a béchamel, then folded in an avocado purée. The mixture was poured into a mould and a gelatinous liquid was poured over it. It was then refrigerated so the gelatin would set up and suspend the beautiful purée.

My chef took the salmon for himself, assigned me the terrine, and we got to work in our little corner of the kitchen. He began making the preparations for smoking a whole salmon, removing any lingering pin bones from the animal's flesh with a pair of kitchen tweezers.

Eagerly, I went to get some gelatin from the supply room, but discovered that all they had was the powdered variety.

Having only used sheet gelatin, I turned the package over to read the instructions. On the back of the box there were what I'm sure were very helpful tips, written in not one but three languages: German, French and Italian. This was when I realised that this wasn't going to be my day.

Rather than asking for help – which I'm not sure I could have done anyway, since I didn't speak anyone's language – I decided, with all the confidence and lack of foresight of an eighteen-year-old, to wing it. I bloomed what felt like the right amount of gelatin, prepared the terrine, set it in on a steel utility rack in the walk-in refrigerator, and left for the afternoon.

This was one of those times when you know you've made a mistake and spend several hours delaying the admission of it, even to yourself. I spent the afternoon in my room, trying to catch a nap, but I couldn't sleep. As I tossed and turned, I couldn't get the image of that green glop out of my mind, and I grew more and more anxious as the afternoon wore on.

When I returned to the kitchen at around four o'clock, I hesitantly went to check on the terrine, fearing the worst. Which was just what I found. Not only had the terrine failed to set, but it was disgusting, with a green slush in the centre of the mould, and an algae-like attempt at coagulation along the edges.

This was the second moment when I could have reasonably raised my hand, admitted my mistake, and salvaged the day. It would have been very simple: we would have let the failed version melt, then added the proper amount of gelatin, and refrigerated it.

Instead, I decided to pop the terrine in the freezer and *force* it to set up.

Now, in most kitchens, the chef will make his rounds before service, checking on sauces and other preparations at the stations at which they are prepared. But at La Terrasse, a kitchen steeped in tradition and formality, we did it a little differently: each cook presented his dish to the chef, then sliced off a taste for his approval.

As the presentation hour approached, I retrieved the mould

from the freezer. It now resembled a partially defrosted, frozen avocado soup, slushy around the edges with a little *granité* island of avocado in the middle. Even the smell of it was bad. It was as if I had accidentally come up with *real* mould, the kind of thing you find in a filthy motel bathtub.

Slowly, shivering with the dread of what was to come, I approached the executive chef, who was giving off his customary glower.

'Chef,' I mumbled, raising up the slimy green creation.

The chef took one look at the terrine and unleashed a fury at me the likes of which I had never heard before. Miraculously, the verbal beating my chef received for not detecting and solving the problem was even worse. It was a tongue-lashing so severe that this grown man was reduced to tears and, unable to recover from the shame, he left for the night.

As a consequence, the executive chef stepped in to cover for him. So this man who had just been telling me to go back where I came from – in a foreign language that, for the first time, I understood perfectly – proceeded to lord over me all night. He ordered me around imperiously, giving me a sneer so sharp I could have cut my finger on it. It was a terrible night. We didn't even try to save the terrine. Instead, the chef instructed me to take a spoon to any solid portions I could find and make little avocado quenelles. The next few hours were a blur of tears and quenelles, a cruel memory set against the echo of the veteran German chefs sniggering in the background.

I expected to be screamed at one last time after service had finished, but at the end of the night, the chef just left me without another word. He went off to a corner of the dining room and quietly savoured a glass of champagne. I wondered how he could enjoy anything after a day in which he had had publicly to savage two of his workers. But now, years later, I understand: the incident was just one event in one day of a chef's life. He had dealt with it and, because he had come up with the quenelle solution, the guests were happy and he was able to move on without a second thought.

When the rest of the crew went out that night to party in the town and usher in the New Year, I staggered back to my room, alone. I felt like the lowest of the low, and didn't want to see anyone.

But here's the thing: that was the night that I could have said screw it and quit. It would have been easy to leave. In fact, it would have been the easiest, most appealing thing in the world. I had left a lot back home, including a girl I loved and a group of teenage friends who were hanging out and having fun in the last days of that time of life when you really have no responsibilities to anyone but yourself.

But I wanted to be a chef. I wanted it more than anything. So I swore to stick it out, to work seven days a week, to get harassed in languages I didn't speak, to do whatever it took to make it.

Over the next two weeks the chef put us on the graveyard shift, a vicious, soul-crushing schedule meant to break us. There were no days off. There was nothing but work, shouting, and more work. I saw lots of other cooks come and go during those two weeks, unwilling to endure it, but I held on. I had made my decision, and there was no going back. I still had a long way to go before I made it, but I knew that, at last, I was on my way to becoming one of those hardened veterans who had come through Victoria-Jungfrau.

Ultimately, I learnt German to near fluency and, against all odds, stayed for two years at La Terrasse, becoming a *chef de partie*. I learnt everything that I would need to carry me on to those French kitchens I had set my sights on, and in time, to New York City.

But as much as I grew in those two years, the most valuable lesson was the one that took place while I was absorbing that harsh German punishment on New Year's Eve 1989. That was the moment when I resolved never to give anyone reason to speak to me like that again. It's a strange, backward-seeming motivation for such a noble profession – taking inspiration from the desire not to screw up – but like I've said, cooking is at heart a lonely business, and you do whatever it takes to get through the day.

————————————

What do you eat for breakfast?
Yoghurt with cereal and banana.

What dish would you cook in order to seduce someone?
I wouldn't.

What do you never cook?
There is a Swedish dish from up north called *surströmming*, fermented herring.

What's the one dish you find hard to get right?
Iniera bread: an Ethiopian pancake-like sourdough bread that you eat with every meal.

White Lie
DAVID BURKE

The chef/owner of davidburke&donatella, David Burke first rose to prominence at New York's River Café. He then went on to become executive chef of Park Avenue Café and vice president of Culinary Development for the Smith & Wollensky Restaurant Group. Burke trained at the Culinary Institute of America and alongside legends such as Pierre Troisgros, Georges Blanc and Gaston Lenôtre. He has been a part of several American Culinary Gold Cup competitions, was voted Chef of the Year by his peers in America in 1991, and was the first non-Frenchman to win the Meilleurs Ouvriers de France Association medal and diploma, France's highest cooking honour. He is the creator of several gourmet packaged goods and the author of Cooking with David Burke.

SEVERAL YEARS BACK, one of my customers, a real nice lady, told me that she wanted me to cater a fiftieth-birthday party for her husband. They were an artistic pair, with friends in the arts and entertainment field, and she flattered me right into it: 'We love your food. It's unique and different, and I know you'll do something that'll make him happy. Please, won't you do it?'

How can you say no to that?

The details were manageable: 200 people. A huge rented event hall with a decent kitchen. A couple of hors d'oeuvres, two main courses to choose from, dessert. The usual.

I said I'd be happy to. Hell, it'd be my honour.

And *then* she tells me that there's a hook. The birthday boy loves surprises, and is a soufflé fanatic, and she wants to combine these passions, blowing him away with a giant floating island – the classic French dessert that features clouds of meringue adrift in a sea of custard – his favourite thing in the world. She envisioned an island big enough to serve 200 rolling into the room as the climax of the celebration, the pièce de résistance.

I didn't know how in the world I was going to make such a thing, so as we shook on it, I said what any good chef would say, 'No problem.'

I had to be out of town for a few days just before the party, so my team and I had a planning meeting. We went over the canapés, the meal, and then came up with a pretty straightforward strategy for the dessert. The pastry chef would make twenty enormous meringue clouds and bake them. Then we would press them together and, simply because of the tacky nature of meringue, they would stick to one another. Finally, we'd transfer them into the biggest bowl we could find, surround the island with crème anglaise, shower it with mint and powdered sugar, and float candles in the crème.

We weren't going to serve this thing, mind you. No, no, no. We were going to wheel it into the hall on a cart – like a wedding cake, if you will – let everyone sing 'Happy Birthday', then wheel it out. Behind the scenes, we'd have already made 200 individual servings, ready to be presented in their ramekins. Everyone would think that the giant island had been divvied up; in reality it would just be thrown away.

On the day of the party, I was about to board an aeroplane back to New York, when one of the guys called me on my cell to tell me there was a problem with the meringue.

'Don't worry about it. We'll deal with it when I'm on the ground,' I said, and hung up. How bad could it be?

Arriving at the banquet hall that afternoon, I was impressed. My customer had spared no expense, turning it into an elegant dining space, with white linens, exotic floral centrepieces and a very sexy lighting design.

But when I left this little paradise and pushed through the door into the dark kitchen, I saw that the meringues had all collapsed. They were flat and big as manhole covers, and totally useless.

I turned to my pastry chef. '*And*,' he said with the grin of one who thrives on adversity, 'there ain't no more egg whites to be had.'

He knew what he was talking about. It was a Sunday, and a few of the cooks had made a trip to all the markets in the immediate vicinity, only to discover that they had been mercilessly picked over, with maybe a carton or two of eggs remaining per store.

There's some genetic thing that chefs have. A perfectionist gene, I guess. I could have done something easy to get out of this predicament. I could have piled up the 200 finished servings in a big pyramid, lit the hell out of it with candles, and probably everyone would have been happy. It wouldn't have been a *Guinness Book*-worthy floating island, but it would have worked fine.

However, one of my customers had ordered a floating island, damn it, and I was gonna give it to them.

'We have to do something,' I muttered to myself. 'This is the pièce de résistance. We have to do something . . .'

I stood there, eyes closed. Thinking. All the while feeling the gaze of my team upon me . . .

'OK, I got it!' I said, and my crew's eyes lit up. Here was the quick thinking they expected from their leader.

But what I said next was definitely *not* what they had planned on: 'Everybody, bring me your dirty laundry. Aprons, towels, chef coats, whatever.' I paused, then clarified: 'As long as it's white.'

I went over to our supply table and found the big white garbage bags we used to clean up after ourselves at events like this. I walked around, holding the bag open wide with both hands, like somebody taking a collection, and the guys threw all their linens inside.

We loaded the bag into the enormous bowl that was supposed to have the meringue in it, teased the plastic to create little meringue-like wisps, and poured the crème anglaise around it. Then we dusted it with powdered sugar and mint leaves, and lit the floating votives that were standing in for birthday candles, setting them afloat in the custard.

It looked just like it was supposed to – a giant floating island – even though it was really a miniature garbage barge.

Right before we wheeled this decoy out into the banquet hall,

I instructed my guys to stand around it and sing 'Happy Birthday' along with the other guests. Their mission was two-fold: one, to provide a security detail for the barge, making sure nobody touched it; and two, to sing at a really fast clip, so the song would be over and the island out of sight as quickly as possible.

We walked out into the room singing 'Happy Birthday' and everybody stood up and cheered, oohing and ahing at the sight of the beautiful floating island. As soon as the last speedy note had been sung, my guys helped the guest of honour blow out his candles. He maybe blew one out himself.

Then we ran the cart out of the room and into the kitchen. We dismantled it immediately, just in case someone came back looking to take a picture or something.

The desserts were served and nobody was the wiser. It was a triumph of on-your-feet thinking, if I do say so myself.

I'm still pretty friendly with that woman, and her husband. I never did tell them about the secret of the floating island, though if they see this, the jig is up.

Well, she *did* say that he loved surprises as much as he loved meringue.

Surprise!

What do you eat for breakfast?
Cereal with Flavor Spray or fruit with Flavor Spray or English muffins.

What dish would you cook in order to seduce someone?
Scrambled eggs with lobster and caviar or spoons with caviar
wrapped in goldleaf.

What do you never cook?
Fiddlehead ferns and anchovies.

What's the one dish you find hard to get right?
Brown-sugar desserts.

Neverland

BILL TELEPAN

Born in New Jersey, Bill Telepan attended the Culinary Institute of America, then worked in a number of the best restaurants in New York City, including Gotham Bar and Grill, where he was sous-chef for several years, Daniel, and Le Bernardin. He also spent six months working under the great Alain Chapel at his restaurant in Mionnay, France. He was executive chef of Ansonia on New York's Upper West Side and of Judson Grill in midtown Manhattan, where he received three stars from the New York Times. *In 2005 he opened the restaurant Telepan. He is the author of* Inspired by Ingredients: Market Menus and Family Favorites from a Three-Star Chef.

A BIG REASON I love being a chef is all the stuff that goes with it – the unusual working hours, the palling around with other chefs and cooks, the horsing around in the kitchen.

Don't get me wrong. I love food, and I take the food itself very seriously. But being a chef means that, on some level, you don't have to grow up. You may have perfectly normal adult relationships outside the four walls of your workplace, but when you don your apron and step into your arena, it's like entering a professional Neverland.

This is, I believe, a distinctly American phenomenon. You certainly don't find it in European kitchens, a lesson I learnt early in my career.

In 1990, I was a twenty-three-year-old cook, and I was doing great. I had been to the Culinary Institute of America and I was working in a well-regarded restaurant in New York City, paying my dues as a line cook. I loved my work and felt that I was on my way to wherever I wanted to go.

But something was missing. I had never been to France. And the more I got to know about the best American chefs, the more I realised that they had all worked in France at some point in their careers. They talked about those days with awe and romance. Clearly, something magical happened over there that took their understanding of food and their craft to a new level.

So one day I decided to take the leap, move temporarily to France, and spend some time working in a three-star Michelin restaurant.

I've always been self-reliant, maybe to a fault. Rather than asking for help from one of the chefs I knew, I made the securing of a job overseas into my own personal pet project. I wrote a letter in English, had it translated by a woman I knew who spoke French, and then had it double-checked by the teacher of my weekly French class. I then handwrote thirty copies of the letter, addressing them to the nineteen three-star Michelin chefs at the time, and eleven highly regarded two-star chefs.

The responses were not encouraging. In fact, twenty never bothered to respond at all. Five said I'd have to pay them for the privilege of working in their kitchen (fat chance). Four said no.

The single favourable reply came from Alain Chapel, a three-star master chef, who said I could work for him at his eponymous restaurant, but that he wouldn't pay me and that I'd have to stay for two years.

I made the necessary arrangements and set off to France, arriving by train in Mionnay, about twelve miles north of Lyon. As I stepped on to the platform, I looked every bit the brash American cook, with my leather jacket, T-shirt and pack of smokes.

I turned up at Chapel's restaurant in the middle of the afternoon, and what I saw when I opened the door floored me: it was the day before the restaurant was to reopen for the new year and Chapel himself was actually dining with the staff; they were all sitting in the dining room, in their starched kitchen whites, having lunch and sipping wine.

I had never seen anything so civilised in my entire life.

Chapel noticed me standing there and, before I could introduce myself, he asked me to leave, telling me to come back tomorrow, 'when the work begins'.

I was embarrassed and scared, and I tore out of there.

I was also uninformed. What time *was* the right time? I came back the next day at eight o'clock, but it turned out I was an hour late. Fortunately, Chapel hadn't arrived yet and, determined not to be sent away twice, I dived in and started helping out. Nobody questioned my presence – or offered me any direction. I didn't really know what to do, so I tried to look busy, my confusion only enhanced by the setting, which was overwhelmingly elegant: there were fresh flowers on all the tables, silver trays at the waiter stations, and in the kitchen the equipment was flawlessly maintained, from the unmarred copper pots and pans to the Le Creuset casseroles.

It didn't matter that I had spent three years in one of the best restaurants in the United States – I felt like a total ignoramus.

Out of the eighteen cooks, two were Japanese, two were Belgian, and the rest were French. But no matter their nationality, *none* of them wanted anything to do with the dumb Yank who had shown up in the middle of lunch the day before and then come late again that morning. They probably thought I'd be gone for good by the end of the day.

Soon enough, Chapel drove up with his little truck, bringing fruit, vegetables, meat and fish from the market, as he did several times each week. These market runs are legendary, . . . and for an American like me it was an epiphany to see this chef's profound connection to local farmers.

I joined the other guys, helping to unload the truck, trying to blend in and look like I knew what the hell I was doing.

Finally, Maurice, the *chef de cuisine* – a refreshingly soft-spoken guy for a French chef – introduced himself and assigned me to the fish station, the *poissonnier*.

I didn't really enjoy my first month at Chapel. I might have been part of the fish team, but I never touched a single fish. Instead I would make tomato *concassé* (coarsely chopped tomatoes), pick herbs from the restaurant's garden, and act as a runner, retrieving stuff from the walk-in refrigerator.

I got to know the walk-in very well, and I must say that there were things about it that fascinated me. I was used to big stainless-steel refrigerators back home. This one was a small box, about 10 feet long and 5 feet wide, and it was made even smaller by the wooden shelves that lined its walls, reducing the area in which you could move to a slender 2½-foot aisle. The shelves popped in and out of little holes that made it easy to remove them for cleaning – a charming and old-fashioned touch.

I was fascinated by how well organised and immaculate the walk-in was. Stocks weren't stored in big white buckets like they were in US kitchens, but in stainless-steel canisters. The fruit and vegetables, some of them still in crates from the market and caked with dirt, were plumper and more vibrant than any I had seen. In the back was the fish and meat, arranged neatly enough for a photo shoot.

But as much as I respected the treasures of the walk-in, I wasn't satisfied with the work I was doing. I had been a line cook back home and here I was relegated to basic prep work.

One of the reasons I was so underutilised was that often, especially during lunch, there were more employees than guests. It wasn't unusual to do just four covers for lunch, or sometimes none at all. There'd be more than a dozen cooks in the kitchen and not one person in the dining room.

An additional reason for permanent residency on the bench was a cook on the fish station whom I'll call Sushi Guy. He was from Japan, and had been referred to Chapel by a well-regarded sushi master. At first I found him impressive and intimidating – he had beautiful sushi knives and did all the butchering. But in time I came to almost hate him. Though he never said a word to me, his message was clear: I'll take care of the fish, New Guy, you deal with the petty stuff. And he was usually so proficient that he didn't need any assistance. But one day he was hopelessly backed up, so I got my knives and my cutting board and set up next to him, preparing to give him a hand. He turned towards me, muttered something in Japanese, and pushed me away – literally shoved me backwards with the palms of his hands.

I tried to explain that I was trying to help, but he wouldn't have any of it. He just gave me an intense stare, made marginally frightening by the knife in his hand.

I was so offended that I wished we were back home so I could wait for him out back after work and have a good old-fashioned street fight with him. But we didn't do that kind of thing in Mionnay.

Things got better, though, thanks largely to a big-hearted guy named Bernard. An accomplished cook at just twenty-five years of age, Bernard was French but spoke English and wanted to practise his English on me. Our station's *saucier*, he would let me help him, teaching me all kinds of classic sauces. Best of all, he instructed using English – until Chapel caught us. 'No, no, no,' he scolded Bernard. 'English is the language of politics. French is the language of cuisine.'

So Bernard and I spoke French from then on. By that time we were friends anyway. His acceptance was like a stamp of approval. One by one, the others started to befriend me. First among the converts were the other fish guys, Anton and Ernest. Then came the two Belgians, Carl and Xavier, big, strapping guys who worked the meat station, along with a seven-year veteran of Chapel's kitchen named Freddy. Carl and Xavier were as goofy as they were huge – well over 6 feet tall – and they loved to make fun of the lone American.

'You stupid American,' they would say, shaking their heads in mock contempt. And I'd answer back, 'If it wasn't for us Americans, you'd be speaking German!' Then Carl and Xavier would crack up, laughing their big meaty chuckles. It was a routine we did at least once a day.

Eventually I got on well with everyone in the kitchen, including the pastry guys – though I can't remember their names – and the *other* Japanese guy, Mitzu, a great cook with an infectious grin and a great sense of humour. I loved singing to Mitzu; my favourite song was a faux-Irish number that I serenaded him with every day: *His name was Mitzu, oh Mitzu, O'Reilly*.

So, once the ice was broken, things were great for me at Chapel. I loved waking up in the morning and coming to work, then going out with the guys after the dinner shift. I even saw my enemy, Sushi Guy, humbled. One night after service I was going out to a *moules-frites* joint with the Belgians and Sushi Guy forced himself on us, tagging along without an invitation. We got crazy-drunk, and Sushi Guy spent the entire night out of control, fighting off bouts of nausea and being unbelievably loud and undignified – bursting out in laughter one moment, and looking like he might pass out, or throw up, the next.

In the morning, when we got to work, Sushi Guy sheepishly tried to apologise to us and explain himself. Big mistake. We really didn't care; if anything, his night of debauchery had humanised him. But in apologising, he firmly established himself as King Geek of the Universe and his clout in the kitchen plummeted. Even in a French kitchen, it's possible to be too square.

By the third month, I was as at home at Alain Chapel as I ever was in New York or New Jersey. Maybe *too* much at home . . .

One day, things in the kitchen were particularly laid back. It was one of our dead days for lunch, and all morning Anton, Ernest, and I were picking on the Belgians.

'Hey, shut up, you stupid American.'

'You know, if it wasn't for us stupid Americans, you'd all be speaking German right now.'

'Ha ha ha ha ha.'

This had been going on for hours when I went into the walk-in to get some fish. Carl and Xavier were in there and as soon as they saw me, they started up with the whole stupid-American routine again.

I was so at ease by this point that I had totally reverted back to my childhood self – which wasn't really that far in the past anyway.

I stepped up to Xavier, pulled his arm towards me in a wrestling manoeuvre, spinning him round and getting him in a headlock from behind. As he struggled, we both twisted round, grazing one of the shelves. Its contents bounced violently, then settled.

At some point during my struggle with Xavier, Anton and Ernest had wandered into the walk-in; the next thing I knew, Carl and Ernest were going at it. They weren't punching each other – there was barely enough room in there to throw a decent haymaker – no, they had grabbed each other by the shoulders and were grappling for control. Finally, Carl managed to gain some momentum and thrust Ernest into the back of the walk-in. The shelves there – built for easy removal – broke away, like in an action movie where staircases and windows explode on contact. I remember thinking, like a little kid, how cool that was, and I let Xavier push me into the shelf behind me so I could be like a superhero myself. Sure enough, as I connected, the shelves in my path gave way: rectangular plastic containers of perfectly chopped shallots, carrots, and celery came crashing down to the ground, spilling their contents all over the place.

Carl spun around to witness Anton coming up behind him, ready to avenge the downing of Ernest.

'Yaaaaaah!'

But Carl was already in full flow. He caught the charging Anton like he was a ballerina and flung him aside. *Those* shelves crashed next and buckets of stock – clear vegetable, chicken, veal – fell to the ground, bursting open on contact, and splashing all over the ground.

It was an all-out food fight – the Fish Guys versus the Meat Guys – but, instead of throwing food at each other, we were throwing each other at the food.

Through all of this, Xavier and I were still struggling for dominance, spinning round and round, and each time we grazed a shelf something else would be knocked over. Finally, I twisted him too hard and we lost our balance; we crashed into an overturned crate of herbs, collapsing on the floor.

'The Fish Guys win!' I shouted. 'We still have one guy standing.'

'No fair, you stupid American, there's three of you and only two of us.'

We could've probably argued all day, but suddenly Carl's face froze. Anton and I turned around to see what he was looking at.

Maurice, the *chef de cuisine*, Chapel's lieutenant, was standing in the doorway of the walk-in, shaking his head sadly from side to side.

'Chapel's going to be here tonight,' Maurice said, all business. 'We have a lot of reservations. So you better get going and clean this up.'

Then he left. It was as merciful a response as I could imagine. None of us took our lunch break that day. While the other cooks left to enjoy the afternoon, we stayed to clean up the walk-in, wiping down the walls and mopping the floor. And we busted our butts to catch up, making quickie stocks and slicing fruit and vegetables so fast that it's a miracle one of us didn't lose a finger.

As well as we did, we were still a little behind: a few things were unready for service that night. So when Chapel showed up, Maurice was forced to tell him what had happened. The master was very cold to us that night – it was a quiet, harsh evening in the kitchen.

I left Chapel after six months, when my money ran out and I needed to get back home to some paying work. I stayed in touch with many of the other cooks. We wrote to each other for years, before we moved on to other friendships, to families, to – dare I say it? – our adult lives.

I still hear about them once in a while. A few years ago, a couple I know returned from the Riviera and were telling me about the restaurants. There was one they hadn't made it to, a little place in Provence run by a hot young Japanese chef they had heard about named Mitzu.

'I know him!' I said, then started singing: *His name was Mitzu, oh Mitzu, O'Reilly.*

I broke off, lost in a memory of that kitchen, those guys, and our daily taunting and torments, our little playpen in the back of a three-star Michelin restaurant.

When I came to, my friends were looking at me like I was nuts.

'Sorry,' I said to them. 'You were saying?'

What do you eat for breakfast?
I eat yoghurt with granola, cornflakes and multigrain flakes.

What dish would you cook in order to seduce someone?
I seduce my wife with a bowl of linguini with white clam sauce.

What do you never cook?
There is nothing I never cook – I'll try anything.

What's the one dish you find hard to get right?
There have been some dishes I couldn't get right, so I've erased them from memory.

The Curious Case of Tommy Flynn
JONATHAN EISMANN

Jonathan Eismann is the chef-owner of South Beach, Florida's perennially hot Pacific Time restaurant, which has been at the centre of the Lincoln Road scene since the restaurant was launched in 1993. A graduate of the Culinary Institute of America, Eismann began working professionally with Pan Asian flavours in New York City in the 1980s as chef of the Acute Café on West Broadway, and then at such restaurants as Batons, Fandango, Mondial, and China Grill. In 1994, he became one of the first chefs to receive the Robert Mondavi Award for Culinary Excellence.

T HERE ARE MANY differences between a chef and a cook. A chef, in a competitive big-city environment anyway, needs to have vision, create his own dishes, and manage a crew of peripatetic soldiers. He needs to be able to stay calm under pressure, navigate any number of thorny political situations, and be able to recognise and coddle the media.

A cook doesn't have to do all that. A cook has to do one thing: execute, execute, execute – the same dishes, over and over, all day, every day, for months if not years at a time. Some cooks want to be chefs, and that's fine. But ambition isn't a job requirement, at least not in my kitchen. I'm looking for guys who can cook well and consistently and are willing to work their butts off.

I've always put a premium on hard work. Back before I owned my own place, you could find me right alongside the contractors, painting, tiling, and woodworking. Even when it comes to my own place, I'm happy to come in on, say, Christmas Day, and refinish the floors.

I respond to this work ethic when I encounter it in others. I'm not making any judgements about people who don't have it, but when I see it I'm drawn to it.

Which is how I came to hire a young line cook named – for this story, anyway – Tommy Flynn.

This was in 1989. I had been the chef at restaurants such as Mondial and Fandango, and most recently China Grill. I was planning to open my own restaurant down in Miami – Pacific Time on Miami Beach – which I eventually did. To bide my time, and make a living, I took a low-profile gig as the chef of a ninety-seat Victorian-style café way up in nosebleed land in the East Nineties on Madison Avenue.

The restaurant was really a glorified bar typical of the Upper East Side. If you've been to or read about Jim McMullen's or J. G. Mellon's, then you know the kind of place I mean. The menu was perfunctory, but I created and executed it with pride. In fact, we were once written up in *Gourmet* magazine for our burgers.

Across the street from this restaurant was a small epicurean shop fashioned as a mini-Balducci's: dark-wood panelling, fresh fruit and vegetables piled artfully in crates, and lots of imported condiments and delicacies. They also had a sandwich counter from where I often bought my lunch.

This is where I met Tommy, a short, scraggly, pimply, red-headed, working-class Irish kid from Queens. He was about twenty-five years old and an intense worker, especially compared to the preppy but lethargic neighbourhood kids alongside whom he worked.

Tommy had great New York sandwich-counter style. He'd slap your sandwich together in record time, always making it exactly the same way – with just the right proportion of meat to cheese to salad to bread – then snap open a paper bag with one hand – I still remember the quick 'pop' it made as the air was forced into it – and pack it up for you.

I didn't know Tommy that well. Because of the counter that was always between us, I had actually never seen him from the chest down or even shaken his hand. But I admired his work ethic.

You're constantly losing employees in a restaurant kitchen, so one day I decided to stroll across the street and casually poach young Tommy. Having watched him work for months, I had no doubt that I could teach him what he'd need to know to be a cook in my five-man kitchen.

In return, I thought, I'd earn his loyalty and have a guy on board who wasn't always on the lookout for the next job.

We spoke. He took the job. We set a start date. And I stopped going to that shop for my sandwiches, a small price to pay if my plan held true to form.

When Tommy showed up in my kitchen a few days later, he pretty much looked like what I'd expected him to when he left the confines of his counter.

Except for one thing. On his left arm was a device: a tan-coloured cuff of sorts around his wrist, with opaque plastic appendages that stretched under and around his knuckles. On his forearm was a lever; whenever he wanted to open or close his fist, he had to crank the lever to manipulate his hand.

If you had a GI Joe with action grip as a kid, then you get the idea.

I took one look at that device and felt terrible. This kid had left his job for me and I was pretty sure that I had screwed him up bad. Surely, he could never work in a professional kitchen.

'Tommy, I don't know what to say. There's no way you can work here, man.'

Tommy had obviously been down this road before. 'Listen, boss,' he said. 'Don't worry about it.'

He went on to explain that he had gotten trashed on beer one night and fallen asleep on his arm, cutting off the circulation for hours. As a result, he had put his nerves to sleep.

He continued, with sunny optimism, to explain. 'The doctor said I was really lucky. A few more hours and they would've had to amputate it.' Twice a week he was going to a Queens clinic for therapy, but it obviously wasn't doing any good.

I subsequently learnt that this injury presents itself in drunks and junkies all the time. Not that Tommy was either.

To convince me of his physical dexterity, he began grabbing, lifting and putting down a series of pans and utensils. Even though he had to crank the lever each time he picked something up and again to release it when he put it down, he had such a rhythm about it that he was, it seemed to me, faster and quicker than most guys in my kitchen.

OK, I thought, let's give the kid a shot.

It turned out that Tommy was exactly what I had hoped he would be: a great executor. All you had to do was show him how to make a dish – explain what the signs of doneness were, what to look and sniff for, and how to plate it – and he was good to go.

And he had great instincts. For example, many young cooks who aren't blessed with natural finesse miss the centre of the plate, by which I mean they will put down the protein, the starch and the vegetable, and when all is said and done, there'll be a big white portion of plate showing through in the middle. Tommy didn't have that problem; he naturally filled out the centre, making it that much easier to train him.

Over the next few months, he worked the sauté station, then the fry station.

One Sunday, we were grinding our way through a typically long, gruelling brunch. The kitchen was hot – so hot that we all wore shorts in the summer – and Tommy was flowing to his own unique rhythm, a series of traditional kitchen movements punctuated by his emphatic, though strangely silent cranking of the hand lever.

As if brunch weren't enough of a circus, we had to keep producing a ridiculous amount of toast to go out with the entrées. As a result, we had five or six toasters lined up along the lowboy – a waist-high stainless-steel shelf – and periodically, when they were all going at once, they would overload the outlet. I'd have to stop everything and run over and play around with the cables, or reset the breaker, until they came back on.

As I was making my way over for the umpteenth time, Tommy said, 'Chef, if you want, I'll come over there and fix that for you.'

I told him to just stay where the hell he was and do his job.

What was he, crazy? How could he tackle an electrical problem with that crazy contraption on his hand?

Tommy pulled a New York City Electrical Union worker's card out of his wallet and flashed it at me.

'Chef, I'm an electrician. I can fix that.'

As always, Tommy was full of surprises.

I handed him my needle-nose pliers and stood aside. He hopped up on the lowboy, his exposed knees on the steel, and went to work on the socket.

'Tommy,' I said. 'You're the electrician, but that thing's hot. There's 220 volts running through it.'

'Don't worry, Chef, I –'

And then a deafening boom rocked the room and the kitchen went pitch black. A few seconds later the emergency lights came on and washed the room in their B-movie glare. All the cooks were standing round, rattled. But Tommy had vanished.

Then I heard a noise from the ground, like the crying of a sick baby goat. I looked down and saw Tommy in a heap, a crumpled bundle with a little pile of red hair on top. He had been blasted right off the lowboy.

'Oh my god, Tommy. Are you all right?'

Not a word. Just more wounded groaning.

I dispatched one of the line cooks to call EMS and knelt down beside the kid.

'Tommy! Are you OK?'

He began to nod unconvincingly.

'Are you OK?'

'Yeah. Yeah.'

'What's your name?'

'Tom . . . Tom . . . Tommy.'

'Let's try to get you up.'

I hooked my arms under Tommy's armpits and helped lift him up off the ground. He put his arms out, one against the lowboy and one against the door to the walk-in.

Suddenly, he snapped into consciousness, his eyes locked on the door.

No, not the door.

His left hand.

It was open, and as he stood up on his own two feet, he held his hand out before him, like an infant just discovering that it was attached to his arm. He opened and closed his fist . . . without the aid of the lever.

'Chef! My hand. It's fixed. It's fixed.'

He continued opening and closing his palm with delight. Laughing.

'I can't believe it! It's fixed!'

He took off the device and threw it in the garbage can, flexing his hand again and again, faster and faster.

'It's totally back to normal!'

Of course it was. Because, Tommy later told me, his biweekly therapy consisted of a technician attaching electrodes to his hand and forearm and zapping them with little bursts of electricity. If only they had turned it up to a near-lethal dose, he might've been spared all those months with a semiprosthetic hand.

His paralysis cured, Tommy got back on the line and went back to work. He was a little thrown at first – not having to crank that lever disturbed the rhythm he had established over the past few months. But Tommy was a great cook, an intrepid professional, and he adjusted soon enough, pumping out dish after dish just the way I always knew he could.

What do you eat for breakfast?
Whatever my five-year-old leaves on her plate.

What dish would you cook in order to seduce someone?
Breakfast in bed the morning after.

What do you never cook?
Casseroles. I just hate the whole idea.

What's the one dish you find hard to get right?
Roast goose.

Acknowledgements

First and foremost, we thank the chefs, for your time, stories, and honesty. Obviously, without you, there'd be no book.

Thank you to Karen Rinaldi, for judiciously entertaining all possibilities; Panio Gianopoulos, for your smart editing, quick turnarounds, and good advice at every step of the way; Eleanor Jackson, David Forrer, and Alexis Hurley, for your excellent cheer and relentless dedication to getting it all right; and, for your invaluable assistance and support, Lindsay Autry, Phillip Baltz, Jennifer Baum, Dan Bignold, Thomas Blythe, Bob Bookman, Tony Bourdain, Juli at El Bulli, John Carlin, Rachael Carron, Samantha Clark, Mel Davis, Catherine Drayton, Scott Feldman, Rea Francis, Richard Green, Dan Halpern, Irene Hamburger, Gabrielle Hamilton, Susan Kamil, Chantal Keller, Sean Knight, Bill Knott, Pam Krauss, Lizzie Kremer, Shelley Lance, Mark Lawless, Carol Macarthur, Ellen Malloy, Gary Morris, Stephen Morrison, Aline Oshima, Anna Elena Pedron, Amy Pennington, Liz Ravage, Leah Ross, Felicity Rubinstein,

Chiki Sarkar, Lori Silverbush, Belinda Smith, Lee Tulloch, Zoe Waldie, Christa Weaving, Araminta Whitley, Kimberly Yorio, and Laura Yorke.

– K.W. and A.F.

Personal thanks to my mother, who encouraged me to try everything; my father, who finds the bright side of every catastrophe; Harry Ptak, for always being there to help; Andrew Friedman, for making this collaboration such a pleasure; my colleagues at Inkwell, for their abundance of faith; and Mhelicia Sarmiento, for helping to get my family to the table every night.

– K.W.

My heartfelt thanks to Kimberly Witherspoon, for coming up with a great idea and inviting me along on the adventure. This was a terrific partnership and a lot of fun. And to Colin Dickerman, for remembering me from way back when; David Black, for your constant counsel and friendship; Caitlin Friedman, for making life easy and miraculously fun, even during the home stretch; and Declan and Taylor: you two couldn't have picked a better time to start sleeping through the night.

– A.F.

A NOTE ON THE EDITORS

Kimberly Witherspoon is a partner at Inkwell Management, a literary agency based in Manhattan. She is very proud to represent four of the chefs in this anthology: Anthony Bourdain, Tamasin Day-Lewis, Gabrielle Hamilton, and Fergus Henderson. She and her family live in North Salem, New York.

Andrew Friedman is a writer who specialises in all things culinary, with a focus on chef and restaurant culture. In addition to his own work, he has co-authored more than a dozen cookbooks with some of the most successful chefs and restaurateurs in the United States, including Michael Lomonaco, Pino Luongo, Alfred Portale, Bill Telepan, and Tom Valenti. He lives in New York City with his family.

A NOTE ON THE TYPE

The text of this book is set in Linotype Sabon, named after the type founder Jacques Sabon. It was designed by Jan Tschichold and jointly developed by Linotype, Monotype, and Stempel in response to a need for a typeface to be available in identical form for mechanical hot metal composition and hand composition using foundry type.

Tschichold based his design for Sabon roman on a font engraved by Garamond, and Sabon italic on a font by Granjon. It was first used in 1966 and has proved an enduring modern classic.